WIND AND SEA OBEY HIM

Approaches to a Theology of Nature

ROBERT FARICY SJ

SCM PRESS LTD

© Robert Faricy 1982

334 01792 0

First published 1982
by SCM Press Ltd
58 Bloomsbury Street, London WC1

Typeset by Gloucester Typesetting Services
and printed in Great Britain by
Richard Clay (The Chaucer Press) Ltd,
Bungay, Suffolk

WIND AND SEA OBEY HIM

This book is dedicated to
Père Gervais Dumeige SJ,
with great respect and appreciation

I want to thank warmly Sister Lucy Rooney SND for helping me with the manuscript in several ways, Jesuit Fathers Francis A. Sullivan, Gerald O'Collins, John Navone and Paul Steidl-Meier for reading it and making suggestions, and Mrs Leslie Wearne for translating chapter I from the original Italian and for typing the entire manuscript. I am grateful to all of them for their patience and encouragement.

Rome, Easter Sunday 1982   *Robert Faricy SJ*

Contents

Note to the Reader

Regarding the Christian attitude towards nature, we find two possible models in St Benedict and St Francis of Assisi.

The monks of the monastery of Monte Cassino, which was founded by Benedict, followed his Rule (which has become a model for monastic life) and learned to administer the earth by making it yield intensively, without, however, causing it to lose its fertility. Following the Rule of St Benedict, Cistercian monks were to have a wide influence in Europe, particularly in draining marshes, deforestation, cultivation and the use of hydraulic power. Benedict and his tradition represent the ecological aspect of the Christian attitude to nature, the attitude of responsible service.[1]

St Francis, on the other hand, represents the aspect of praise and contemplation. When he saw the beauty and greatness of nature, Francis praised the Lord, and he left us his 'Canticle of the Creatures':

Praise be to you, my Lord, with all your creatures,
Especially for master Brother Sun,
Who illuminates the day for us . . .
Praise be to you, my Lord, for Sister Moon and the stars.
In heaven you have formed them, shining, precious, beautiful.
Praise be to you, my Lord, for Brother Wind,
For air and clouds, clear sky and all weather,
Through which you give your creatures sustenance . . .
Praise be to you, my Lord, for our sister Mother Earth,
Who sustains and cares for us,
Bringing forth various fruits and coloured flowers and herbs.

Both models, of course, are authentically and correctly Christian. And I have tried here to take into account the Christian attitudes that they represent. This book, then, does not pretend to be a 'theology of ecology', nor a manual for finding God in nature, but, I hope, something of both. I have tried to present the main elements of a theology of nature.

Not, then, an 'ethics of nature'. Ethics deals with values; systematic theology considers meanings. One reason why we have today such a weak Christian ethics of nature lies in the fact that a Christian theology of nature has not been sufficiently developed. This book hopes to make a modest contribution toward such a theology.[2]

A theology of nature should cover far more than do the following pages and even more than a much larger book could cover. Since putting a complete theology of nature in one book appears too ambitious, and perhaps impossible, I have tried here simply to take different theological approaches to nature so as to sketch out certain aspects or facets of nature in different theological ways.

The first chapter looks at the relationships between God, nature and us in a somewhat general way, as those relationships hold in the Bible and in the Christian tradition. The second chapter considers the same relationships – between God, nature and us – in terms of dialectical process, not Hegelian dialectic, but Marxist. I should add that any orthodox Marxist, of whatever school or persuasion, might well be horrified at what I have done with the formal dialectic of Marxism. I have used it as a convenient and, I think, the best available set of categories to interpret St Paul's letter to the Romans, chapters 5 to 8, in a contemporary process framework. Chapter II, then, sees God, nature and us interacting in dialectical process.

The third chapter treats the problem of evil, the dark side of nature, in itself and in our misuse of it; nature as menacing and dangerous, nature as perverted by human lawlessness. The approach here is, in part, by means of dealing with certain apocalyptic images, in part a reflection on biblical texts and in part apologetic (in the classic sense of a Christian *apologia*). The fourth chapter concerns nature's transformation in art and what this means for the Christian artist as a *model* for all Christians in their relationships with nature. The last chapter takes up different ways of finding God in nature through service, praise, thanksgiving, contemplation, meditation or reasoning, and seeing in nature metaphors for the humanity of Jesus Christ.

What do I mean by the word 'nature' as I use it here and in the following chapters? I mean, first of all and primarily, nature in the sense of the natural elements, nature as not yet transformed through human work of some kind. But I do not want to exclude our own nature, human nature from the concept of nature. Nor do I want to exclude nature as changed, transformed, put into new forms, by human work. 'Nature', then, in this book means *principally* nature as distinguished from us and from our work that transforms it; but 'nature' in a secondary sense includes us and the products of our work with nature. The exact meaning of the word, of course, will depend on the context.

Nature itself is mysterious, a mystery. We can know more and more about it, but we can never fully understand it. The best approach to nature is that of Job: humility in the knowledge that we understand very little about it.

> Then the Lord answered Job out of the whirlwind: . . .
> 'Where were you when I laid the foundations of the earth?
> Tell me, if you have understanding . . .
> Have you commanded the morning since your days began? . . .
> Have you entered into the springs of the sea? . . .
> Have you comprehended the expanse of the earth?
> Answer, if you know all this . . .'
> Then Job answered the Lord:
> 'Behold, I am of small account; what shall I answer you?
> I lay my hand upon my mouth . . .
> I have uttered what I did not understand, things too wonderful
>   for me, which I did not know . . .
> I repent in dust and ashes' (Job 38.1–42.6).

I

'And God saw that it was good':
God, Nature and Human Responsibility

'What, according to the Christian tradition, is our relationship with the natural world, with nature?' Since we ourselves belong to the natural world, the question asks, 'What relationships exist between nature as a whole and that particular part of nature we designate as "human"?' The answer, then, will include not only our relationship with the natural world outside ourselves, but also our relationship with ourselves and with one another as belonging to nature. We can look for the basic elements of the Christian view of the person-nature relationship in the Bible.

The Old Testament: Genesis 1.1 to 2.3

Old Testament theology situates the relationship between person and nature within a comprehensive theology of the relationship between the Creator and his creation, within a theology of creation. This theology of creation permeates the whole Old Testament, but we find it especially in the Wisdom literature, in the prophetic books and – condensed into a creed, a profession of faith – in the first chapter of the book of Genesis.

Genesis acts as the introduction to the Old Testament and the first part of the book of Genesis (Gen. 1.1–2.4) serves as a sort of prologue to the entire Old Testament. This document is a creed, a theological statement of Israel's faith in a good and ineffable God who is Creator and Lord of the world and who transcends his

I

creation. To underline God's transcendence with regard to what he creates, this profession of faith uses as a principal image the spoken word (Gen. 1, passim). For example, 'And God said, "Let there be light"; and there was light' (Gen. 1.3); 'And God said, "Let the waters under the heavens be gathered together into one place, and let the dry land appear." And it was so' (v. 9); 'And God said, "Let there be lights in the firmament of the heavens to separate the day from the night; and let them be for signs and for seasons and for days and years, and let them be lights in the firmament of the heavens to give light upon the earth"' (vv. 14–15). The idea of creation by means of the spoken word preserves and accentuates the radical distinction between God and the object of his creative action. The creature is not an emanation of the divine nature, nor a necessary reflection of God's own being. The only continuity between Creator and creature is the word of God. His very word is creative: 'God said, . . .' Therefore, all of creation belongs to God because it is produced by his word.

The credal document of Genesis employs a means even more important than God's word to stress the divine transcendence, the fact that God is wholly and infinitely other with respect to his creation: it de-divinizes all creatures. The document shows God's transcendence by underlining that creatures are in no way divine. Only God is divine; only God is God. There is no other God outside of the God of Israel. The Creator is absolute Lord of all things that he has created, because he has created them; and created things are simply what they are – creatures.[1]

Light, for instance, is the first thing God creates. It is a cosmic light, symbol of God's creative presence, the light-space in which the divine act of creation takes place. Light is created before the creation of the celestial bodies, separately from the sun, moon and stars. In this way, the sun and the moon, which in mythologies are often living beings and in some way divine, are de-mythologized, de-divinized, made natural, seen simply as creatures. Also, Genesis, chapter 1, reacts against the cultural atmosphere of the nations around Israel, an atmosphere saturated with astrological beliefs; the stars are stripped of all divine meaning and magic power. The sun,

2

the moon and the stars do not create light. They are just mediators of the light that was created before they existed.

In the theology of creation of Genesis 1, the theme of de-divinization occupies a central place. Creatures are in no way divine. They are merely creatures, not divine, infinitely distant from their ineffably transcendent Creator and completely subject to him as to their Lord. This subjection is brought out in the fact that God gives creatures their names and he assigns them their roles. 'God called the light Day, and the darkness he called Night' (Gen. 1.5). God says, 'Let the earth put forth vegetation, plants yielding seed, and fruit trees'; and the earth does so because the Creator has ordered it to (vv. 11–12). Behind the earth's fertility, and causing it, we do not find the sun or the moon, or, as in many myths, the tree of life. We find only the creative word of God.

Not only is nature radically distinct from God, but it belongs to him and it is good. This goodness of creation is not a moral or aesthetic quality; rather, it is order, the harmony of the universe in all its elements. What God creates has order, is good, has value, precisely because God has created it and holds it in existence. The goodness and value of every creature depend totally on God; yet they are properly the goodness and the value of the creature itself. 'And God saw that it was good'; the sentence runs like a refrain through the document. 'And God saw everything that he had made, and behold, it was very good' (v. 31).

Creation is good because it is in covenant with the Creator. The idea here of God's faithfulness to his creation comes, by extension or a kind of projection, from the concept of the fidelity of Israel's God to his people. Just as God has chosen Israel, forming a people out of the chaos of slavery in Egypt, so God created the world, making it emerge from a primordial chaos, forming it into a cosmos, an ordered universe. Like Israel in covenant with God, so too all of creation and every creature depends on God, comes under his lordship and has its proper place and role to fulfil. Again, the dependence of Israel on God gives Israel as a people its value. God did not choose Israel because of its beauty or fidelity or greatness or goodness, but only out of love. The book of Wisdom speaks of the Creator's love that calls things into existence:

> Yes, you love all that exists, you hold nothing of what you have made in abhorrence, for had you hated anything you would not have formed it. And how, had you not willed it, could a thing persist, how be conserved if not called forth by you? (Wisd. 11.21–26).

When the text of Genesis 1.1–2.4 comes to the creation of human beings, the introduction, 'Let us', indicates a more personal and intimate creative activity on the part of God. Nevertheless, we stand clearly in the ranks of the creatures. The emphasis on God's transcendence undergoes no diminishment. There is simply, on the one hand, creation – including us – and, on the other hand, God.

'Then God said, "Let us make man in our image, after our likeness; and let them have dominion over the fish of the sea, and over the birds of the air, and over the cattle, and over all the earth"' (Gen. 1.26). Unlike other creatures, we are created in the image and likeness of God. The use of two words that reinforce one another, 'image' and 'likeness', emphasize that we, the image, correspond to the original, God. The notion of image, for a nation that forbade images of God and reacted strongly to the idols of its neighbours, is startling, and it is meant to be. God is not only transcendent of us, but very near to us. 'Image' here is a parallel idea to that of 'covenant'; both express God's closeness to us. Just as Yahweh commits himself in covenant to Israel, and with covenant fidelity to all creation, here he commits himself specially to the whole human race. We have a special relationship with God. God's transcendence is only one side of the story; his nearness to us is the other. And yet we are in no way divine: we, too, are creatures.

As a result of God's having created us in the image of God himself, we have dominion over the other creatures. We are masters of nature and responsible for it. The passage concerning the human creature as the master of plants and animals is also present in many creation myths; in the creation myths, however, it serves to introduce the fundamental precept, 'You are to take or to destroy nothing in nature except what is necessary for your daily subsistence.'

4

This precept is significantly missing in the Genesis document. Again, the entire tone and sense of the text is anti-mythological. We are masters of the plants and animals *because* we are in the image of a transcendent and all-powerful God, the Lord of all things, ourselves and plants and animals included. So, then, not only nature is de-divinized, but also our relationship with nature. In creation myths, nature belongs to God or to the gods; we are part of nature and may take and use only what is necessary, for it is not really ours. In the Genesis document, however, although nature belongs to God, God has made us in his image and given us dominion over nature.[2]

It is not we who are related to God through nature, but nature that is related to God through us. Nature, having been de-divinized, is nevertheless related to God; it receives the dignity of being under God's sovereignty through being under our sovereignty. We are responsible to God for the world and the rest of the world is related to God through us. Nature is now completely de-divinized. Nature has been shown to be radically distinct from God and we have been distinguished from nature. In this way, the view of reality that is presented here is a complete departure from the mythical view of reality. The world has no magical power to save us or to destroy us; the power belongs to God. A fearful and awe-filled attitude towards the world has been replaced by a matter-of-factness about the world, and magic has been replaced by prayer. Thus we are freed from nature and nature itself is freed for our use.

Both we and nature are de-divinized and freed for progress. This matter-of-factness about both us and nature is the pre-condition for the development of science, for technology and for social, political and economic progress. No progress is possible except to the extent that we can face the world without intimidation. This is not to say that we are free to exploit nature; our task is to take care of and to build the world, exercising the dominion given us by God, carrying out our stewardship.[3]

Since the Bible is normative for Christians, we can at this point formulate a first thesis: *as Christians we understand nature as good but as non-divine and we take responsibility for nature because God has put us in charge of it.*

The Christian sees nature as good, but not divine. There is no Christian 'mystique' of nature. Nature, in the Christian perspective, is looked at with a certain responsible pragmatism. The Christian's appreciation of nature's beauty and goodness does not result in a set of sacred taboos with regard to nature, but in a matter-of-fact sense of responsibility towards it.

The New Testament: John's gospel and the letters of Paul

In the Old Testament, God's word is a metaphor. The New Testament takes the concept of God's word and identifies the Word of God as Jesus Christ. For example, in the letter to the Hebrews, Christ is identified with the prophetic and creative word of God. 'In many and various ways God spoke of old to our fathers by the prophets; but in these last days he has spoken to us by a Son, whom he appointed the heir of all beings, through whom also he created the world' (Heb. 1.1–2).

John's gospel, especially, identifies the word of God with Jesus Christ and this identification becomes the central concept of an elaborately developed christology. The christology of John's gospel has many dimensions; one of these dimensions or aspects might be called the cosmic dimension. However, for John, it is not Christ who is cosmic, but the cosmos that is christic. The gospel presents the universe as rooted in Christ, as coming to be through him and as finding the fullness of its perfection only in and through him.

The initial reference to the beginning of the first chapter of Genesis, 'In the beginning', leaves no doubt that the prologue of John's gospel talks about the same creative word of God as does Genesis, but in a new way and in the light of a great new fact: that this word has become flesh and dwelt among us. And, like Genesis 1.1–1.4, the Johannine prologue is a theological creed, a profession of faith, that announces in a somewhat abstract form the theological lines of development of the main and narrative part of the gospel. The theme of the first eleven verses of John's gospel, the first half

6

of the prologue, is that God's creative word, the word he spoke 'in the beginning', the word that is God and that is with God, has come into the world to dwell among us. God, ineffable and transcendent, has taken flesh and become an element of his own creation, immanent in the world. John's prologue uses the same image, the word of God, that the first chapter of Genesis uses to affirm God's transcendence. Here, however, the image of the word, without losing its previous meaning, is used to express the *immanence* of God, in Jesus Christ, in the world.

God is present in Jesus and 'we have beheld his glory, glory as of the only Son from the Father . . . full of grace and truth' (John 1.14). In the Bible, 'glory' is the sign of God's presence, and 'grace and truth' reflect the traditional attributes of the God of the Old Testament, his compassionate love and his faithfulness. In Jesus, God has entered into his creation and is immanent to the world.

In the Old Testament, God is understood as absolutely transcendent and the world as non-divine. This de-divinization of nature is a basic premise, or prime requisite, for technology and political and social progress. However, de-divinization, as such, tends to lead to de-personalization. When nature is de-divinized, 'there is the tendency to de-personalize it'.[4] This tendency is overcome in the New Testament. In the theologies of John and Paul, God's transcendence is still maintained, although he is now understood also as immanent to the world in Jesus, and the world is understood in a personalistic way, as personalized in Christ. This personalization of the world in Jesus Christ is particularly marked in the writings of Paul.

There is general agreement that when Paul speaks of the church as the body of Christ he is speaking realistically and not metaphorically. In some mysterious way the church *is* the body of Christ. St Paul does not explain this, but simply states it as a fact. What he is affirming is the organic relationship between Christ and Christians, in that Christians constitute the body of Christ.

Paul also asserts the organic relationship between Christ and the whole universe (a subject on which there has been little theological research). He enunciates the same doctrine as that found in John's

7

gospel: that all things were created and exist in Christ. However, the viewpoints and theologies of John and Paul are not the same. John describes the progressive fulfilment of the cosmos through man's faith response to the Word of God; his theology is elaborated within the framework of the great metaphor of the word – of dialogue and the interpersonal relationship of language, of words which are pronounced and to which one responds. Paul, on the other hand, sets forth the progressive fulfilment of the cosmos through the incorporation of all things into Christ; his theology of Christ and the world is elaborated within the framework of the organic relationship of everything which exists to Christ.

For Paul, everything comes from God; all the things which exist are created by God. 'O the depth of the riches and wisdom and knowledge of God! . . . For from him and through him and to him are all things. To him be glory for ever. Amen' (Rom. 11.33–36). But everything comes from God *in Christ*: 'There is one God, the Father, from whom are all things and for whom we exist, and one Lord, Jesus Christ, through whom are all things and through whom we exist' (I Cor. 8.6). There are four passages in the writings of St Paul which are especially important in this connection and in which he states that everything which exists subsists in Christ. Let us take a look at these four passages.

Paul's teaching with regard to the relationship of the world to Christ is found in the first chapters of his letter to the Ephesians and the doctrine of these chapters is summed up in two short passages:

For he [the Father] has made known to us in all wisdom and insight the mystery of his will, according to his purpose which he set forth in Christ as a plan for the fullness of time, to unite all things in him, things in heaven and things on earth (Eph. 1.9–10).

And he [the Father] has put all things under his [Christ's] feet and has made him the head over all things for the church, which is his body, the fullness of him who fills all in all (Eph. 1.22–23).

Right from the beginning, God's plan is centred on Christ, and this plan has not yet been wholly fulfilled but is in process of fulfilment,

8

so that, starting from the beginning and ending when the course of the ages is complete, all things will be recapitulated in Christ. And the church has a central position in this plan. Christ is the head of the church and it is through the church that God's plan is manifested. Moreover, although the church is the body of Christ and hence, so to speak, the main area of his active presence, he is nevertheless actively present through the whole universe. This doctrine of the progressive fulfilment of God's plan and of the central position of the church in this plan may seem very modern to us. However, its basis can be found in the rabbinical literature of Paul's period. God continues his creative activity: he creates in the beginning and also today, and, furthermore, the centre of his creative activity is his people.

This same view is also found (although slightly differently expressed) in the letter to the Colossians 1.13–2.15 and particularly in a passage which sounds like a hymn:

He is the image of the invisible God,
the first-born of all creation;
for in him all things were created,
in heaven and on earth, visible and invisible,
whether thrones or dominions or principalities or authorities –
all things were created through him and for him.
He is before all things,
and in him all things hold together.
He is the head of the body, the church;
he is the beginning, the first-born from the dead,
that in everything he might be pre-eminent.
For in him all the fullness of God was pleased to dwell,
and through him to reconcile to himself all things,
whether on earth or in heaven,
making peace by the blood of his cross (Col. 1.15–20).

This hymn is one unified whole. Paul says that all things past, present and future are rooted and united in Christ. This is a difficult statement to understand, but it is what he says.

Verses 1.21–2.15 of the letter to the Colossians form a type of commentary on this hymn, in which two main ideas are linked together. First, Christ is the head of the church and the church is his body. Secondly, Christ is the head of the cosmos and the cosmos is his body.[5] ('In him the whole fullness of deity dwells bodily' (Col. 2.9) – this is a reference to the cosmos as the body of Christ; the word 'body' here refers to the cosmos.) The church thus has a cosmic character and also a central position in the cosmos. Christ is the head of the church and, in a different but analogous way, also of the cosmos – in which the church occupies a central position. Despite the fact that Christ is the head of the cosmos, all things are not already recapitulated in him. They are recapitulated in an inchoate and rudimentary way, but the working out of the reconciliation of all things in Christ takes place within history. Thus, for Paul, creation and redemption are two aspects of one great mystery – the recapitulation of all things in Christ. Creation and redemption are found united in the process of the progressive reconciliation of all things in Christ.

A parallel concept to that of the cosmos as the body of Christ is the idea of the *pleroma*, or perfection or fullness: 'For in him all the fullness of God was pleased to dwell, and through him to reconcile to himself all things' (Col. 1.19–20). In St Paul's writings, the meaning of *pleroma* seems to be that all things are created in Christ, reconciled in him and find their fulfilment in him, in whom there is the fullness (*pleroma*) of God and also, in some way, of everything which exists. In some way everything depends, so to speak, on Christ, and finds its meaning and its very existence in him.

The link between the cross and the resurrection is clear and strong in the writings of Paul. In his letter to the Philippians he shows that the incarnation and the cross are linked with the cosmos through the resurrection:

Have this mind among yourselves, which you have in Christ Jesus, who, though he was in the form of God, did not count equality with God a thing to be grasped, but emptied himself, taking the form of a servant, being born in the likeness of men. And being found in human form he humbled himself and became obedient unto death, even death on a cross. Therefore God has highly exalted him and bestowed on him the name which is above every name, that at the name of Jesus every knee should bow, in heaven and on earth and under the earth, and every tongue confess that Jesus Christ is Lord, to the glory of God the Father (Phil. 2.5–11).

Paul uses this 'hymn' to exhort the Philippians to humility, encouraging them to be imitators of Christ who was the servant of others. Apart from its exhortative function, this passage also tells us that the incarnation implied living out the consequences of the incarnation. For Christ, this entailed his passion and his death on the cross. Abasing himself, Christ entered wholly into the cosmos; he descended into the heart of the cosmos so that, exalted in his resurrection, he could be the Lord of the cosmos. In order to become the central element and focal point of the process of the universe in his risen form, Christ had first to become a part of that process. The world is held together by the risen Christ, but in order to live again he had first to die and, in order to die, he had first to be born. The reason for the incarnation and the passion is the resurrection. The summit – or, better, the deepest point – of Christ's going-out-of-himself, his self-emptying or *kenosis*, is his death on the cross. On the cross he descends wholly into the heart of the universe so as to become, in his risen life, the heart of the universe. By means of his incarnation and death, Christ descended into the world so that he might draw the world to himself.

The teaching contained in the letter to the Romans 8.18–25 adds a further aspect to those of the three texts already considered: the doctrine that the whole world – human beings and also *nature* – is in some way the object of God's salvific love.

I consider that the sufferings of this present time are not worth comparing with the glory that is to be revealed to us. For the creation waits with eager longing for the revealing of the children of God; for the creation was subjected to futility, not of its own will but by the will of him who subjected it in hope; because the creation itself will be set free from its bondage to decay and obtain the glorious liberty of the children of God. We know that the whole creation has been groaning in travail together until now; and not only the creation, but we ourselves, who have the first fruits of the Spirit, groan inwardly as we wait for adoption as sons and daughters, the redemption of our bodies (Rom. 18–23).

It is thus the whole creation which is the object of salvation in the plan of God. The hope of mankind is the hope of the whole of creation. The creation and the redemption are indissolubly linked. Everything created was created in order to be saved and is the object of redemption, and this includes the whole cosmos. Paul places the salvation of the cosmos, of everything which has been created, within the context of our salvation, and especially within the context of our resurrection, that is, of the redemption of our body. We can thus distinguish two clear points here: (1) the salvation of everything which has been created is a consequence of our salvation; and (2) nature itself is not simply an instrument of our salvation but is also in some way the object of redemption.

We can now formulate a second thesis: *as Christians, we understand nature as personalized in Jesus Christ risen.*

The Christian understands nature as centred in the risen Christ. Jesus Christ risen is the focal point of the Christian religion and also the future focal point of the convergence of history. The world and its history belong to the Lord and everything is held together in him. Jesus is not only the future goal of the world but is also, through his universal influence, immanent to the world. Nature is thus personalized because it is rooted in Christ.

The present-day debate: the influence of the Judaeo-Christian tradition in the field of ecology

In recent years, a debate has begun as to the practical consequences of the Christian view of the world and there has been particular speculation as to the Christian origins of the attitude towards nature of abusive exploitation. Is the Christian concept of the relationship between us and nature wholly or partly (and if so, in what way), or not at all, the basis of a conception of nature which leads to pollution and the irresponsible employment of natural resources – in other words, the treatment of nature not as a garden but rather as a mine to be exploited?

It is true that 'polluting, exploiting the land for mere speculation, wasting resources, and placing all-out consumerism at the centre of life all mean a lack of respect for others of this and future generations, . . . in fact, the exact opposite of loving one's neighbour'.[6] However, the debate is concerned not so much with the morality of present-day exploitation of nature but rather with the origins of the concept of the relationship between us and nature which is behind such an attitude and which acts as its conceptual basis.

The debate started with an article by Lynn White, in which the author deplores the ecological consequences of the Christian ethic which places emphasis on our authority over nature.[7] Other authors have since written along the same lines, although sometimes with different shades of emphasis, asserting that an anthropocentric and aggressive attitude towards nature is derived from the Christian idea of human sovereignty over all other creatures and that the Judaeo-Christian tradition has unfortunately produced a blind science and technology and an insane economistic culture.[8] Christianity is accused of preaching 'the absolute right of sovereignty over nature'.[9]

Basically the criticism is that in some way Christian tradition concerning our relationship with nature, based as it is on Old Testament doctrine and in particular on that found in the first chapter of the book of Genesis, has contributed to a certain de-personalization of nature and to a lack of respect for it. Given the divine declaration of our unilateral and absolute sovereignty over nature, in Western culture, with our Judaeo-Christian formation, we have exploited the earth, wasting its resources and polluting it.

Such generalizations are of course subject to qualification. Large-scale exploitation of the earth began only in the last century (following many centuries of Christianity), when industry and science converged to produce the technological revolution, which is literally changing the face of the earth. Moreover, the view that some

Christian idea is at the basis of the concept or viewpoint which leads to the exploitation of nature idealistically, presumes that ideas have a great influence on human behaviour. However, human experience would tend to show that, on the contrary, concepts are frequently used not to start a course of action but rather to justify it once it has been started.

In any case, many authors, most of them theologians, have defended Christianity against this accusation. They have in particular shown that Christian teaching on the relationship between person and nature leads not to exploitation but rather to the responsible development of natural resources and the judicious administration of the earth, not as a mine to be exploited, but as a garden to be tended.[10] This debate has been developed mostly among Protestant theologians – which should give us pause.

The fact is that there is a difference in the conception of the person-nature relationship between Reformation Protestantism and Catholic tradition (which is here taken to include the Roman Catholic church, the Orthodox churches, and the Anglican church). This difference interests us here. Although I may run the various risks inherent in generalizations (risks which are particularly great in the religious field), I should like to sketch out a Catholic reaction to this debate.

The main influence on the conception of the relationship between person and nature in present-day North American culture (and almost all the authors taking part in this debate are from North America) is probably to be found in Luther's doctrine of the 'two kingdoms'. In the Lutheran view – as, indeed, in that of much Protestant theology – the kingdom of Christ and the kingdom of the world are seen as in tension, in some sort of mutual opposition or antithesis. There is a similar antithetical tension between God's government of the world with power and his rule of grace by means of the gospel, between the world and the church and between the order of creation and that of salvation. The Christian is thus in an antithetical position with regard to nature. A large section of Protestant tradition has seen God's mandate to man to rule over his surroundings in the light of this theology of the two kingdoms. The result has been a tendency towards an exploitative relationship with nature, a working *against* nature.

I would in no way deny that Luther and the whole Lutheran tradition show a deep feeling of appreciation of nature and of God's presence in nature. However, the Lutheran perspective, in which there is a relationship of paradox, opposition or dialectical tension between human nature and grace, has certain consequences as concerns the relationship between us and nature.[11] On the other hand, when nature and grace are seen as in synthesis, as in Catholic tradition (especially in the Thomistic tradition and in that of the Greek Fathers), the relationship between us and nature is understood more positively and there is an attitude of working *with* nature rather than against it.

Greater emphasis is placed on the principle of the incarnation in Catholic tradition than in Protestant tradition. God has become truly human and thus matter is the proper vehicle of spirit; material reality is good; human nature is radically good; and nature, although de-divinized, possesses a religious value. Nature must be used, developed and built up, but its laws must also be respected.

It seems obvious to me that Protestant tradition has never encouraged irresponsible exploitation of nature; on the contrary, this tradition today places great emphasis not only on our sovereignty over nature but also even more on the commandment to care for it. This is the concept of 'stewardship', which might be described as 'management with a strong sense of responsibility'.

The problem lies in the fact that the concept of stewardship, or of a strong sense of responsibility for nature and towards other members of the human race, present and future, is not enough. Obedience to the commandment is not enough, even in theory. The de-divinization of nature must be balanced by a view in which nature is seen as rooted in Jesus Christ risen. This is the Catholic interpretation of the Pauline theology of the relationship between Christ and the world; however, such an interpretation becomes impossible within the framework of the Lutheran theology of the 'two kingdoms'.

In Catholic, as against Protestant, tradition, the main reason for an attitude of responsibility towards nature is not obedience to the divine commandment given in Genesis; that is, it is not *primarily* obedience, which takes the form of stewardship. It is, rather, love for Jesus Christ as present in nature with his universal influence, and love in Christ for other people, present and future. This is a love which unifies, creating union among persons, between persons and nature and between persons and God, all in Jesus Christ.

We can conclude this chapter with a third thesis: *we can, as Christians, have an attitude towards nature that – combining responsible stewardship with a strong love for nature and for all creation as grounded in Jesus Christ – promotes ecological balance and helps overcome our alienation from nature in a relationship of union and harmony.*

II

'All creation groans':
The Holy Spirit, Nature and Society

The first chapter considered God-person-nature relationships
especially in the light of certain key biblical texts and also in terms
of recent discussion of Christian attitudes towards ecological problems. This chapter goes further in that it will take up our relationship with nature not simply as a relationship in the present, a
'vertical' relationship, but as a moving and evolving relationship, a
'horizontally moving' relationship in a world in process. The
person-nature relationship will be understood as in dialectical
process.

This chapter then will move on to a consideration of relationships
in society and how the person-nature relationship affects them and
is affected by them. Thirdly, the central section of Paul's letter to
the Romans will be interpreted so as to lead to a better understanding of our relationship with nature and with other persons in the
framework of Christian life in the Holy Spirit.

Nature in theology

In contemporary theology there exists a failure to come to grips
with the relationship between human beings and the natural world
of which they are a part. Theological considerations of the person-
nature relationship, even where they can be found in the literature,
tend to see that relationship as static, not as a dynamic relationship
that includes the processes of our transformation of nature, of the

impact of nature on us, of the transforming effect in us of our working with nature and of the social and political dimensions of our relationship with nature. The principal new theological current of the 1960s, the eschatological current best represented by the German theologians Jürgen Moltmann, Wolfhart Pannenberg and Johann-Baptist Metz, was and remains focused on human history as eschatology. It deals with personal relationship in Jesus with God and with the relationships of human society, but it almost completely neglects our relationships with the natural world we live in. The same can be said of the other important theological contributions since 1950 – of the theology of secularity and of the theology of the word, elaborated by such theologians as Gerhard Ebeling and Ernst Fuchs. The Latin-American theology of liberation of Gustavo Gutiérrez and others, while being open to the study of the person-nature relationship, has never really pursued that study.[1] Like German theology, it operates at the level of history and society.

Theology's failure to account for our interaction with nature has unfortunate consequences, consequences which are becoming more and more evident. In general, contemporary theology has failed to deal effectively with problems that involve our own biological nature and with problems of human ecology. In particular, the increasingly important fields of genetics and genetic research, of human sexuality, of fertility control, of human dying and of the chemical manipulation of human nature, cry out for serious theological reflection. Yet, these fields have been left to the Catholic moral theologians and to the Protestant Christian ethicists, as though they presented only, or even primarily, ethical problems. Again, theological reflection on ecological and environmental problems has for the most part either been relegated to the domain of Christian ethics or has been approached only statically and metaphysically, as in the case of Joseph Sittler's work in terms of nature and grace.[2]

But are not the problems of our interaction with nature ethical problems? Yes, surely. But ethics deals with values and values must be rooted in meaning. And that is the problem. Discussion of values, where the meaning base is weak or non-existent, tends always towards polemical cant. Witness, for example, the theological discussion of the doctrine of the papal encyclical *Humanae vitae*. Granted that the *Humanae vitae* theological aftermath was an extreme case where polemics sometimes even degenerated into ecclesiastical politics, it shows what can happen when ethics does not find a solid and fruitful theological base of meanings. Values follow from meanings. Ethics considers values. Systematic theology considers meanings. What is needed is theological reflection on the Christian *meaning*, the Christian significance, of our relationship with nature.

The theological reflection needed must fulfil certain conditions. First, it must be a reflection on human existence according to this all-embracing dimension: the fact that we are with and a part of nature. Secondly, it must be a reflection on human existence in the light of God's revelation to us in the person of Jesus Christ; for this is, in one way or another, what all Christian theology must do if it is to be Christian and theological.

Thirdly, theological reflection on the person-nature relationship in the light of Jesus Christ must centre not only on what that relationship is but also on what happens, on the relationship as *process*. Nature itself must be understood as historical, as in process, as dynamically interwoven with human society and with society's history and progress. That is, the reflection must be not in categories of being but in categories of becoming, of genesis, of evolution, of change. Any metaphysics of being studies what-*is*; by its own definition and parameters, it cannot study what-is-not; and so it cannot effectively consider what-is-not-yet, the future. But a theology of nature, because it must focus on the processes of our interaction with nature, has to have a process orientation. Metaphysics of being takes a vertical cut through reality to isolate what-is from its becoming, from the processes that make what-is what it is and what it may or will become. What is required is a horizontal approach that understands reality as moving out of a past into a future.

The so-called 'process theologies' of Alfred North Whitehead, Charles Hartshorne, Schubert Ogden and John Cobb are relevant, of course, to this question.[3] And they do take with theological seriousness person-nature interactions. But they work from and within a matrix of a metaphysics that tries, in various ways, to be both a metaphysics of being and a metaphysics of becoming. The history of theology shows that operations that confuse, identify, or try to hold in a kind of union of contradiction both being and becoming simply do not work well. There is no intention here facilely to write off the North American process theologies, but to enter into theological dialogue with them here would go beyond the scope of this chapter.

The double Christian perspective on the person-nature relationship

Speaking generally, it can be said that two somewhat opposed views of our relationship with nature have dominated Christian thought since the time of Augustine. The first is the Augustinian view, which sees mankind and nature as fundamentally in tension, in a certain opposition. As a result of original sin, we are not only alienated from God but also from other persons and from nature. Nature, the 'world', is under God's judgment, fallen. In most Protestant theology of the Reformation tradition, this Augustinian perspective on our relationship with nature goes very deep and is for the most part in line with Augustinianism as influenced by Luther and Calvin.

Probably the most important influence has been that of Martin Luther's doctrine of the two kingdoms. In the Lutheran perspective, as well as in the general perspective of much Protestant and some Catholic theology, the kingdom of Christ and the kingdom of the world are understood as in tension, in some kind of opposition, in antithesis. There is the same antithetical tension between God's rule of power in the world and his rule of grace through the gospel, between the church and the world, and between the order of creation and the order of salvation. Human existence, then, and especially Christian existence, is in antithetical opposition to nature.

The Augustinian tradition, and especially Protestant theology, has read God's mandate to us (Gen. 1.1–2.4), that we exercise dominion over the world, in the framework of this two kingdom theology. The result has been an exploitative approach to nature, a working against nature.[4]

The other important Christian approach to our relationship with nature goes back to Aristotle and appears in the Middle Ages in the theologies of the great scholastics, particularly in the works of Thomas Aquinas, and can be seen today especially in Orthodox and Anglican theology and in much Roman Catholic theology. It shows up in the writings of such diverse thinkers as Teilhard de Chardin and Karl Rahner. It is the view that we are in union with nature. In this tradition, the key principle is the principle of the incarnation. True God has become truly human and therefore matter is the proper vehicle for spirit; material reality (nature) is good; human nature is essentially good; and although nature is not at all divine, it has religious value. We are in union with nature and therefore must work with it, not against it. This is, of course, the background of scholastic natural law theology, of Teilhard's theology of building the world and of Rahner's theology of nature and grace.

These two Christian perspectives are complementary. We *are* alienated to some extent from nature; the contemporary environmental crisis is an example in many ways of that alienation. And, too, we are in union with nature, part of nature.

It is an essential part of our task to overcome our alienation from nature by working with nature through science, technology, industry and social and economic organization. This process we call human progress. It is a dialectical process in that it has dialectical 'phases'. In a first phase we try to overcome our alienation from nature by uniting with it. In a second phase, we work with nature. And in a third phase, we use and enjoy the fruits of our labour. These phases are dialectical; they describe a process – the basic process of the person-nature relationship.

The dialectic of person and nature

Dialectical movement is the movement in time produced by the tension between two elements, in this case person and nature.[5] This tension or polarity is a relationship in which there is always some kind of opposition between the two elements. However, the two opposed elements can be related in two different ways. The two elements can complement one another in a fruitful relationship; in this case, although one element somehow dominates the other, the relationship is one of complementarity. This is true ideally of our relationship with nature.

The other way in which the two opposed elements in a dialectical process can be related is in the classic master-slave relationship; here, the dominating element uses and exploits the other element. These two dialectical relationships, complementarity and master-slave, are the two fundamental polar relationships and mainsprings of all dialectical movement.

Ideally, we and nature are not in a relationship of master and slave but rather in one of complementarity. We dominate nature in a complementary way and the union is a fruitful one. In our working union with nature, we become more human, develop our own humanity. Our union with nature is a humanizing union.

In any positive or complementary union, the elements united are always differentiated. Whether we speak of cells united to form a living body, or of members of a human society, or of the elements that make up any union, true union never confuses the elements united, it differentiates them. In an athletic team, players are differentiated according to the positions they occupy in the team; union differentiates. In friendship, there is, again, a differentiating union. At an even deeper level, marriage is a differentiating union. To the extent that a marriage is a happy and successful union, husband and wife grow as persons. They do not merge or confuse their personal identities; on the contrary, each achieves his or her own personhood – not in spite of the daily lived-out marriage union – but precisely through union with the other person. The differentiation always takes place at the level of the union. Members of a team are differentiated according to function. Friends are differentiated as persons, personalized. In our union with nature, we are united with nature precisely as human, as rational planners and developers and builders. So, in the dialectical process of our uniting with nature, working with nature, producing with nature, we become more human. We transcend our former limitations; we grow; we make more real our own human essence.

The root of the person-nature relationship is need. We need nature, even though we are to some extent alienated from it. This relationship of need is mediated by work; through work, we overcome our alienation from nature in a complementary and fruitful union with nature. Further, we find ourselves in the products of our working union with nature; we see ourselves objectified and exteriorized in the results of our work. In our products, we see ourselves reflected precisely as human and so become more aware of our own nature. This whole dialectical process of our union with and work with nature so as to produce results is also a process of our greater humanization through both the development and the increasing awareness of our human nature.

We are in the image of God. We are creators in the image of the Creator. Our task on earth is to exercise dominion over nature. Dominion is God's, but God has given us a mandate to take care of, work with, develop nature. And in being creative we share in God's own creativity and become more in the image of our Creator; that is, we become more human.

The dialectic of master and slave

The dialectical process of person and nature does not exist in a vacuum: it is interwoven with other dialectical processes based on the relationships of society, on our relationships with one another. Human relationships can be either positive or negative. They can be complementary; when they are, there is a working together towards common goals and something is produced, the fruit of working together. Or a human relationship can be negative. In this case, the relationship is, in some way, one of master and slave; it is not a complementary union but one in which the dominating member uses the other as an object, exploiting the other and appropriating the fruit or product of the relationship to himself.

If human relationships in society and, also, person-nature relationships in technology and industry are positive, complementary, then there is great harmony. In fact, this never occurs. Human relationships in any society are never all complementary; there are always master-slave relationships in which persons use others not as persons, as subjects, but as objects to be manipulated for the greater good of the user. This is the fact of sin.

In the dialectic of master and slave, the 'master' is united with the 'slave' in a working relationship, the work is done principally by the slave and the product goes to the master. Where the two dialectical processes meet is at their common point, that of work. In the master-slave dialectic, the work is done by the slave, who does this work by being in some kind of union with nature, with the material means of production. And this second union is positive, a relationship of complementarity; it is the dialectical relationship of person and nature.

Marxist theory uses its understanding of these two dialectical processes, and their mingling at the point of 'work', to form one complex dialectical process in order to explain proletarian revolution. In a capitalist system, the proletariat is in relation to the owners of the means of production as slave is to master. The worker works and the product goes to the owner except for what is necessary for the worker to keep working. But the worker, in his union with the means of production (fields, tools, equipment and organizational relationships), is in a person-nature dialectical process of complementarity. Thus, the worker is in a humanizing process, becoming more human, stronger and more aware. Theoretically, at a given point, the worker should be sufficiently strong and aware enough of human dignity to break free from the master-slave relationship, overthrowing the capitalist system in favour of a new social and economic order in which the master-slave dialectic does not dominate in societal relationships.

It is at that point, when the proletariat has, through the person-nature dialectic, become strong and aware, that the importance of theory becomes clear. The worker needs to objectify the situation by conceptualizing it so as to understand it. The purpose of Marxist theory (or ideology) is that the worker be able to conceptualize his own situation and so see the possibility of a Marxist revolution.

But is Marxist theory true? Does it really work that way? It seems clear that a great many social phenomena can be explained by a broadly Marxist analysis.

One example is the black civil rights movement in the United States. Briefly, the master-slave relationship that has always in some sense and to some extent existed in the United States between the white population and the black population took the historical form of the structures of racism, including the stereotype of the negro and the traditional Jim Crow institutions. But the black American, in a complementary dialectic with nature in the form of what might be called everyday American life and philosophy, developed and grew in awareness of black identity as (1) a member of a pluralist American society, (2) a Christian and (3) a citizen of a democracy in which everyone should have freedom with opportunity and rights with status. Ideologically, this awareness took the form of (1) black consciousness, consciousness of racial and cultural unity, (2) identification with God's people in exodus toward the promised land (the principal ideological category of Martin Luther King) and with Jesus suffering in and from the sinful structures of society and (3) realization that the black, too, must have freedom, opportunity, rights, status. Objectifying the black situation in ideological categories, and having attained the strength and the awareness to overturn the structures of racism, the American black has accomplished and is accomplishing a social revolution. Marxist ideology, of course, has played almost no role in this revolution; it is in conflict with many of the most important elements of black American ideology. But a dialectical approach does seem to fit and partly to explain the facts.

Other examples of the person-nature dialectic, the master-slave dialectic, and their intermingling at the point of 'work', with the outcome of radical change in social structures, could be taken from the movement for equal rights for women and from most of the contemporary movements for the socio-economic liberation of minority groups.

What has this to do with theology? As has been shown,[6] not only did Marx depend on Hegel to a great extent, but much of the thought of Hegel that most influenced Marx's thinking was a rational, 'de-mythologized' transcription of the main events of the gospel narratives. This means that a Christian should be able to find the fundamental categories of dialectical change beyond Marx and beyond Hegel in the New Testament.

Dialectic in Romans 5: the cross as revolution

The heart of Paul's letter to the Romans, chapters 5 to 8, is not only perhaps Paul's most brilliant theological development, but also contains a double Christian dialectic. This dialectic consists of a master-slave dialectical process, in which the master is sin and we are the slaves, and a dialectic of complementarity between God and man in the saving action of Jesus Christ – a dialectic of complementarity that takes place in the life of the Christian according to the Christian's relationship to Jesus Christ through the Holy Spirit.

Chapter 5 is a unity in itself. It describes what, objectively, God has done through Jesus Christ: our salvation. The three succeeding chapters show how that objective redemption is applied subjectively: the Christian is dead in Christ (Rom. 6) and free from the Law to live in Christ (Rom. 7) according to the Spirit (Rom. 8).

Verses 5–11 of the fifth chapter are an introduction to verses 12–21 and perhaps were intended to be an introduction to all four chapters. It is a brief summary of what follows, with emphasis on God's love for us which is shown by the death of Jesus, which has reconciled us with God and which is poured into our hearts by the Holy Spirit.

Romans 5.12 describes the master-slave dialectic between sin and us. Before Jesus Christ, human existence is in the objective structure of sin; we are the slaves of sin. As a result, we all sin; this is the 'work' that we do. The product of our 'work', of our sins, is death. Verse 13, anticipating verse 20 and chapter 7, speaks of the Law; the Law is the rational objectification of our situation of alienation. It makes things worse in a certain sense. Before the Law, we are not (as) aware of our sinful situation; but the Law, acting as an ideology, rationally objectifies that situation and makes us aware of our condition and of our sins.

Verses 14–20 continue to speak of the dialectic between sin and us as between master and slave, but only in order to bring out, to describe by contrast, the dialectic of complementarity between God and the world in Jesus Christ. God unites himself with us and our world in the incarnation, in the person of Jesus Christ. The 'work' that God does in and through Jesus is 'the obedience of the one man' (v. 19); it is 'what was done by the one man, Jesus Christ' (v. 17). This work is Jesus' death on the cross. The work that God does in union with nature through union with the human nature of Jesus is the work of a dialectical process of complementarity. The dialectical relationship is of the person-nature type. But this work takes place in the context of the master-slave dialectic in which we are situated, in a situation of alienation from God, in which the only wages of our work (sin) are death. Therefore, the work that God does in union with the world (i.e., in Jesus) is a revolutionary work. It is a reversal of structures. The revolutionary work of the cross ends the reign of sin and creates a whole new order of grace. 'Just as sin ruled by means of death, so also God's grace rules by means of righteousness' (v. 21). The revolution of the cross is not so much something Jesus underwent, suffered, as something that he did, a positive act. That act was to overturn the structures of human existence and to create a new order, a new economy of salvation. Chapters 6, 7 and 8 describe the dialectic of our participation in the revolution of the cross and in the new order of grace.

Dialectic and the Holy Spirit

Chapter 6 describes the Christian life as being in the structure of the death of Jesus on the cross. 'When we were baptized into union with Jesus Christ, we were baptized into union with his death' (v. 3). Not only has the old order of sin been overturned by Jesus' death on the cross, but also 'our old being has been put to death with Christ on his cross, . . . so that we should no longer be the slaves of sin' (v. 6). Living in the structure of Jesus' cross, Christians are called to take responsibility, to participate in the work of Jesus, the work of the cross and to be dead to the works of sin. 'At one time you were slaves to sin, but now you obey with all your heart the truths found in the teaching you received. You were set free from sin to become the servants of righteousness' (vv. 17–18). The new life of the Christian in the structure of Jesus' cross leads to eternal life, to the ultimate new order of the resurrection.

Chapter 7 describes the place of the Law in the master-slave dialectic of sin and us; the description is in terms of the individual person, the subject. In Romans 7.7–25, I am seen as alienated from what I ought to be; the self is alienated, not what it should be, not its true self, and so a false self is in control. The Law is the objectification for me of what I should be but am not. In the light of the Law, my alienation from what I ought to be, from my true self, becomes conscious. That is, the alienation is interiorized; I become aware of my *de facto* alienation in a way that I was not aware before I had the Law. 'The Law made me know what sin is' (v. 7). The master-slave dialectical process comes into my awareness, is conceptualized, in terms of what I am and of what the Law informs me I ought to be. A slave to sin, my work is my personal sin; I know from the Law that this should not be the case, but knowledge of the Law only increases my responsibility and so my guilt for the work, the sins, that I do.

Awareness of sin through the Law not only increases guilt but it leads to more sin. I am in an interior conflict between what I am (a sinner) and what I ought to be (faithful to the Law). So I tend to reject what I am, my false self; this, however, is ineffective and solves nothing. So to escape the conflict (although it is a false escape), I reject what I ought to be; I reject the Law; I sin. In this way, the Law multiplies sin. What is the solution to this conflict? 'Who will rescue me from this body that is taking me to death?' (v. 24).

The resolution of the conflict, the overcoming of my alienation from my true self as well as from God, comes about through living in union with Jesus Christ in the new economy of the Spirit; this is the matter of chapter 8. 'What the Law could not do, because human nature was weak, God did' (v. 3). He sent his Son who came with a human nature like our sinful nature so as to 'do away with sin' (v. 4), by overturning the master-slave dialectical structure of our slavery to sin and death by his own death on the cross. He did this so that, in the new order, we can live according to the Spirit, now free from the Law. The Law is the expression of the old situation of alienation, of slavery to sin. In the new economy of grace, the Law is transcended, gone beyond, fulfilled.

Since we now live in the order to righteousness with the life of the Spirit, the work that we now do is according to the Spirit. And it is a work in the revolutionary structure of the cross. The result of our being in the structure of the cross will be that we will also be part of the ultimate new order, the economy of the resurrection, when the revolution of the cross will be completely over and the world to come will begin. The Christian shares the sufferings of Christ now and will share his glory in the world to come (v. 17).

Jesus Christ, by his incarnation, entered the realm of sin, put himself under the Law, and by his death condemned death and sin in his flesh, fulfilled the Law and reversed the structures, triumphing over sin and death and creating the realm of grace and the Spirit. The Christian is baptized into this new structure created by Christ, where death and sin are condemned but still hold sway at the level of the flesh. But the Christian is living in the realm of grace and at death will triumph over sin and death, passing into eternal life, rising with Jesus Christ risen. Even in this life on earth, the Christian is freed from sin and death and under the law of the Spirit; and no difficulties can separate the Christian from the love of Christ (v. 35), for these trials are the Christian's share in Christ's work, the work of the cross.

Continuing a dialectical interpretation of Romans, chapter 8, we can say that in the Christian life we are in a dialectic of complementarity with the Spirit of Jesus, with the Holy Spirit. The dominant role in this dialectical realtionship is that of the Spirit. In other words, the dialectic is similar to the classic person-nature dialectic, but here – rather than a person-nature relationship – there is a Spirit-person relationship. The Holy Spirit is united to us not in a master-slave relationship but in a dialectic of complementarity: 'Everyone moved by the Spirit is a son of God. The spirit you received is not the spirit of slaves bringing fear into your lives again; it is the spirit of sons' (vv. 14–15). The Christian is encouraged by Paul to obey the Spirit, to be docile to the Spirit's guidance (vv. 12–13). The Spirit works in us, helping us in our weakness, expressing our prayer in a way we could never put into words, and producing fruit (vv. 26–27). We already possess the first-fruits of the Spirit's working in us and we look forward to the time of that total freedom that will be the ultimate end-product of the work of the Spirit (v. 23).

Not only we but all of nature have been alienated, have been under the reign of sin and death (vv. 19–20). It is not the fault of creation that it is in this situation, but rather the fault of the one who made it so (v. 20). It seems probable that the 'one who made it so' is not God but mankind; the reference seems to be to Genesis, chapter 2. Sin has alienated not only us from God, and not only us from one another and from our true selves, but also us from nature and even nature from its true purpose. But nature, creation itself, can have hope 'to be set free from its slavery to decay and share the glorious freedom of the children of God' (v. 21). The whole world is groaning to be liberated.

Paul situates the ultimate freedom of creation in the context of our resurrection, in the context of the salvation of our body. The salvation of nature is a consequence of our salvation, especially of the salvation of our body through resurrection.[7] Our working with nature, then, has an eschatological dimension. By uniting ourselves with nature and working with it, by transforming nature, we are in a certain sense 'redeeming' nature.

Christian life and social progress

It is not difficult to put together the person-nature dialectic described in the first part of this chapter with the dialectic of complementarity between God and us in Jesus Christ. In Jesus Christ, God has become incarnate in the world. In his *kenosis*, Jesus, not clinging to his divinity but taking human form, and even the form of a servant, descended into the world, uniting himself with the world; in his death he descended into the heart of the world so that, being raised up, he could, risen, be the heart of the world (Phil. 2.6–11). The salvation of the world begins with the incarnation, which marks the beginning of the work, the mission of Jesus.

The Christian is called to imitate Jesus and so to 'descend into the world', to become involved in the material world, to become involved with nature, at the same time in union with Jesus Christ according to the Spirit. That is to say, the Christian is called to enter into the dialectical structure of the incarnation. This means entering actively into a union with nature, working with nature productively. This person-nature relationship is in the pattern of the God-world relationship in the incarnation and life on earth of Jesus; it is in the pattern of the incarnation. But, because of the sinful structures in the world, this dialectic of person and nature is contaminated by a dialectical relationship between us and the sinful structures of society.

The work that we do in building the world, the work of science and technology and also of social, economic and political organization, is a work that takes place within the structures of human society. These structures are almost always, to some extent, at least partly sinful.

It is true that sin is, above all, in our hearts. But sin within the person has consequences in society. Situations occur which are objectively sinful even though perhaps involving no immediate subjective responsibility on the part of anyone at the time that those situations exist. Sinful structures, social, economic and political, do exist in society; they are objective states of sin. Situations of unjust distribution of wealth, of oppression of various kinds, of starvation, of homelessness, of inhuman living conditions: all these are objectively sinful situations.[8] In a situation of this kind, we are in a dialectical relationship of master-slave with the unjust structures of

31

our existence. We are, to some extent, dominated by them, mastered by them, in slavery to them.

This is the sin-us (master-slave) dialectic described by Paul in Romans, chapters 5 to 8, although here the sin is not within the subject but objective in the structures of our society. We act and work, dominated by unjust structures, and the product of our efforts – other than what might be needed to keep us working or living at a subsistence level – goes not to us but elsewhere.

Yet, in our work activity, we are united with nature in the form of the means of production; this union is a person-nature dialectic of complementarity. At the same time the Christian is united to Jesus Christ through baptism and by grace in a union of complementarity.

Through the teaching of Christianity on social justice, the Christian is able to identify oppressive societal structures precisely as sinful. Furthermore, in the framework of Christian doctrine, I can identify myself as participating, in my daily life and as a Christian, in the mystery of Jesus Christ. This should enable me to assess my own place in society and, with the strength and growth that come from my union by complementarity with, on the one hand, the instruments of production and, on the other hand, my union in the Holy Spirit with Jesus Christ in his church, to work against those sinful structures with a view to changing them, to overturning them.

In this way, the Christian struggle for justice is a participation in the paschal mystery, in the mystery of the life, death and resurrection of Jesus. The Christian lives in the permanent but dynamic structure of the cross of Christ ordered to resurrection. I am called to take up my cross and to follow Jesus, not in the next world but in this one. The cross I am called to carry in discipleship is the cross of involvement in a sinful world, the cross of struggle against the powers of darkness, against all that oppresses us. Seen in this light, the cross is not a symbol of sadness or suppression or resigned defeat. It is a symbol of the struggle against evil, a symbol of the hard work of progress. It is the symbol of victory through difficult toil and pain and suffering.[9]

A reflection on the relationship between person and nature has led to the understanding that the person-nature relationship is dialectical and that it is inevitably interwoven with the dialectical relationships of human society. Dialectical process always involves both person-nature dialectical relationships and interpersonal dialectical relationship. Further reflection has led to the religious significance of dialectical process, to the conclusion that dialectical movement takes place in the categories of the death and resurrection of Jesus.

Inevitably, there is a dark side to our relationship with nature, coloured by sin and leading to the cross. The next chapter pursues this further.

III

The Mystery of Lawlessness:
Nature and Evil

Nature as menacing; nature as perverted

Nature, in all its goodness and beauty, in all its usefulness and in all its harmony, retains an aspect of menace. Nature menaces us. Nature in the form of violent eruptions – storms, earthquakes, epidemics – threatens us. Unpredictable areas of nature can frighten us: the jungle, the arctic wastes, the sea, and sickness, pain and death. Most of all, nature in its form of inevitable death menaces, frightens and confounds us. A theology of nature must consider all this, the dark side of nature, nature in terms not of its order but of its disorder and the harm it can cause, nature as capriciously violent, nature not in its laws but in its lawlessness.

In addition, a theology of nature has to deal with the human misuse of nature, with sins against nature, with nature used not according to God's law but in lawlessness, with our perversion of nature. Through technological progress, we have learned to control nature, to modify it, to develop it. Using nature as a resource, we have made leap after leap in learning to adapt nature to benefit mankind. But these very leaps have a certain ambiguity. Technology, the human adaptation of nature, can be used not only for people but against them. Not that human progress necessarily results in sin. It does, however, result in the possibility of more horrible sins. Freedom through technological progress means greater responsibility. The stakes have risen. The technology that adapts nature to produce nuclear power for heat and light and industry can get dangerously out of hand, as we have learned from breakdowns and leaks in nuclear power plants. Moreover, that same technology produces nuclear bombs; it has given us the capacity to kill more people at once than ever before in history.

The immense complexity of the contemporary person–nature relationship tends to discourage analysis. Still, a broadly sketched picture of that relationship can help in understanding it. Barbara Ward has written:

> For the past four hundred years, the tremendous drives of scientific discovery, of economic innovation and growth, of more and more highly organized natural power have thrust our planet towards a single system of technical and material interdependence. Science has created new energies and new technologies which, harnessed to human purposes, have increased unrecognizably our ability to use and manipulate the Earth's physical resources. Economic ambitions and rewards have as drastically increased the demands and aspirations which people are determined to satisfy. And national sovereignties, armed with these new scientific and economic powers, have thrown a network of trade, of investment of overt or covert political domination round the globe, drawing in the most distant lands to serve as markets, settlements or sources of supply. Thereby they have inexorably created a single, unified, worldwide network of economic and social communication and interdependence. As inexorably they have multiplied the demands and strains upon the planet's depletable resources and upon the delicate biological mehanisms of the shared biosphere. For four centuries we have blindly followed these processes ... *These three vast, undeviating, unremitting pursuits – of knowledge, of economic growth, of national power – have been the fundamental drives of recent centuries.* Like all vast human movements, they bring with them good and evil.[1]

Scientific discovery, economic growth and innovation, and national power have brought forth a situation in which nature, production and economy are interrelated. One would think that the economy should conform to the requirements of a production system that aims at meeting human needs.[2] And that the production system should conform to the requirements of the ecological system, to the exigencies of nature. In fact, the opposite holds true. Nature is violated by the production system, which in turn is determined by an economic system which has almost no respect for nature.[3]

The secularization of nature in Western culture has enabled us to objectify nature, to regard it in a coldly matter-of-fact way so as to work with it. But, in this age, we rarely understand nature as personalized through the incarnation, as personalized in Jesus Christ. And we rarely see our mandate to exercise dominion over nature as a divinely appointed stewardship. Not only do we often not regard nature as related to God through us, but we frequently neglect our own personal relationship with God. No wonder, then, that – when the person-God relationship is not in order – the person-nature relationship equally finds itself in disorder. When we disregard God's law in our own personal life, we fall into lawlessness regarding other people and, also, nature. Our lawlessness regarding nature has repercussions on nature itself; a corrupted person-nature relationship turns nature against us and us against ourselves. We become alienated, not only from God, but from nature and from ourselves.

The fact that God has given us dominion over nature does not mean that the earth belongs any less to the Lord. 'The earth is the Lord's and everything in it' (I Cor. 10.26; Ps. 24.1). Since the sovereignty belongs to the Lord, we must exercise our dominion over nature with respect and responsibility – towards God and therefore towards nature. A study group of theologians has put it this way:

Since God, however, has a moral and rational character, we must in the end submit to things as they are, as a genuine revelation, so far as we can grasp it, of ultimate goodness and wisdom. Hence the careful and comprehensive observation of nature will yield indications for human behaviour which were part of God's intention in creating in the first place, and which therefore have

36

the status of moral imperatives for us. We must ultimately be guided by respect for the intricate character and needs of the natural order.[4]

God's law can be found in nature. Creatures do have a certain structure, in themselves and in their relationship with one another. Nature has a certain order or orderliness which demands study and respect. We can sin against God's law found in nature. We can use nature not with respect and responsibility for the laws the Lord has placed in nature, but in lawlessness.

When we go against nature's ecological laws, we find ourselves alienated from nature, in an ecological crisis. What is sometimes missing is the recognition that the ecological crisis has its roots in alienation from God and in alienation from other human beings. Going against nature includes, and usually begins with, going against God and against other people. Rosemary Radford Ruether puts the relationship between the un-Christian use of nature and the un-Christian use of people clearly:

> [The ecological] crisis has its genesis in certain structures of power and ownership through which the project of industrialization has been pursued nationally and internationally. The exploitation of natural resources does not take place in an unmediated way. It takes place through the domination of labour . . . The abuse of the resources of the earth becomes acute when a small ruling class . . . can use the labour of the vast majority of people to extract these resources, but without having to take into consideration their rights and needs as human persons.[5]

Going against nature has its genesis in opposition to God and, often, in sinful manipulation of other persons. And it always leads to further alienation from God and from other persons.

Sins against nature, that take and adapt nature against people rather than for their benefit, mark the present age like plagues. Human progress has made possible genocide, nuclear warfare, torture as an industry with its own specialists and training schools, the deliberate and government-ratified killing of unborn human life, homosexuality as a mass movement, ecological crises of various kinds and other stupefying horrors that mark this age as modern, that involve not merely 'sinful acts' but whole trends and structures of human society and that cry out to heaven for vengeance, not just because they are evil but because they are organized, planned, technologically sophisticated, massive evil.

Evil today has taken on apocalyptic dimensions. What have we done to God's creation? How have we misused nature? From what quarters can we expect salvation? The appropriate answers to these questions need a framework that does not minimize the gravity of the evil nor the urgency of salvation, a framework that fits the problems, an apocalyptic frame of reference.

The problem involves not only sin, not only the human misuse of nature, but evil in general: suffering and death as well as sin. Some of the evils we see in the world we can explain as rooted in the wrong and sinful use of nature; but other evils, like much suffering and death, appear to be nature taking a threatening form and turning on us.

Let us consider the problem of evil in a perspective appropriate to the dimensions of evil in our times, in an apocalyptic perspective.

Apocalyptic as response to the problem of evil

Apocalyptic is a mode of discourse, a way of communicating that has a characteristic form and a typical content. The Bible contains several examples of apocalyptic: the book of Daniel; Ezekiel, chapters 38 and 39; Zechariah, chapters 12, 13 and 14; the Apocalypse of the New Testament; chapter 13 of Mark's gospel, with the parallel passages in Matthew and Luke.

The form and the content of the apocalyptic manner of speaking or writing or acting can be distinguished but not separated; they go together. Images and symbols and visions, sometimes exotic or bizarre or even grotesque, express a characteristic religious content. The mysterious 'son of man' figure of Daniel, chapter 7, finds an important use in the teaching of Jesus about the end of the world. The separation of sheep and goats symbolizes the last judgment.

The church becomes a woman clothed with the sun and with the moon at her feet.

Apocalyptic differs from prophecy. Prophecy interprets the signs of the present time to point to the future. The prophet sees the outcome of sin and infidelity to God, denounces injustice, calls the people back to their covenant with God and looks beyond present and future evil to deliverance. Prophecy looks to the future that arises out of the present.

Apocalyptic talks rather about the future that breaks into the present. It speaks about God's future for the world, about God's future that breaks into the present. The apocalyptic writer expresses little faith in the present age as at all capable of working itself into God's promised future.

The message of apocalyptic comes through the totality of the apocalyptic writing or action or event; the details are not important. Apocalyptic's message is that the future belongs to God. God is the Lord of history, in charge of the world. The Lord guarantees the future: wrath for the wicked, glory for the just. Apocalyptic sees the future from the standpoint of the future – not as coming-out-of-the-present (as does prophecy) but as supernatural intervention, as divine uncaused-by-world-events action. Apocalyptic speaks of the future as such and as God's; thus, it communicates the hidden. The future lies hidden in the Lord's hands because it belongs to him; he holds the future and makes it present now in a hidden and mysterious way through apocalyptic (which means 'revelation' or 'unveiling'). Symbols and images provide the necessary vehicles for what remains by its nature mysterious and perceived only in symbol.

Apocalyptic states that God controls history. He is not indifferent to suffering, to injustice, to pain, to evil in the world. History has meaning; the world has purpose; the Lord himself will bring history to its final goal. John Navone writes:

The apocalyptic theology of history is a response to the problem of evil.'

The prophetic hope for the moral and physical transformation of the present order has not been realized ... History appears to be so dominated by evil that it can no longer be considered as the scene of God's kingdom ... There is no apparent prophetic explanation for the evils of the present age. The hegemony of the godless demands a new interpretation of history, and apocalyptic theology provides the answer ... God alone can put an end to the evils of history.[6]

Human freedom, dignity, responsibility, are to be taken with maximum seriousness. Apocalyptic shouts against injustice, against the persecution of God's chosen, against sin and wickedness and misery. The image of the last judgment expresses human responsibility, that we do choose and that ultimately we pass judgment on ourselves through our actions.

Apocalyptic confronts evil squarely, even fiercely. Its strong vision of God's final victory makes possible a clear vision of evil in this world. The anti-Christ, a strong apocalyptic figure, incarnates the principle of 'anti-God', of evil. Belief in the reality of the devil and of demons comes from the apocalyptic tradition which, in fact, tends towards a kind of dualism. The strong emphasis on the reality of evil could imply a Manichean dualism were it not for apocalyptic's stress on the omnipotence of God, on his active power, on his universal lordship.

The goal of history is the establishment of God's kingdom at the end of time by God himself. The Lord in his power will bring about the New Jerusalem, the world to come. This does not really detract from the value of human initiative and effort. The efforts and fidelity of those who adhere to God are integrated into God's plan and into the final deliverance (e.g., the seven letters to the churches in John's Apocalypse).

In the Old Testament, the establishment of God's kingdom will come in the last times, on the 'Day of the Lord'. Then, at the coming of the kingdom, God will pour out his Spirit (Joel 3.1–2). In the New Testament, the last times are upon us and the kingdom is already present in Jesus. The eschatological Spirit, the Spirit of the end-time, rests on Jesus, anoints him to overcome evil. In the

Nazareth synagogue, Jesus applies verses 1–2 of Isaiah, chapter 61, to himself:

> The Spirit of the Lord is upon me, because he has anointed me to preach good news to the poor. He has sent me to proclaim release to the captives, and recovering of sight to the blind, to set at liberty all who are oppressed (Luke 4.18).

When John's disciples come to ask Jesus who he is, they find him curing 'many of diseases and plagues and evil spirits' and giving sight to the blind. He answers them:

> Go and tell John what you have seen and heard: the blind receive their sight, the lame walk, lepers are cleansed, and the deaf hear, the dead are raised up, the poor have good news preached to them (Luke 7.22).

Jesus' healings serve as apocalyptic signs of the presence of the future kingdom of God in Jesus. They reveal that the power of God overcomes evil, saves, heals. That the kingdom is here in Jesus is clear from the fact that he acts in the power of the Spirit, the Spirit of the last times and the beginning of the kingdom.

If the theological significance of Jesus' exorcisms, and of exorcisms today for that matter, has been neglected, the reason is theology's neglect of apocalyptic as a category worthy of reflection. Jesus casts out evil spirits because the Spirit of God is with him in power, God's Spirit of the last times breaking in now and triumphing over all. 'But if it is through the Spirit of God that I cast devils out, then know that the kingdom of God has overtaken you' (Matt. 12.28).

And if theology has neglected the existence of Satan, of evil spirits, of personalized forces of evil in the world, even in the face of overwhelming biblical data and Church teaching, this again marks contemporary theology's failure to come to grips with apocalyptic. Church teaching, on the other hand, has regularly referred clearly to the existence of the devil and of devils.[7] In 1972, Pope Paul VI spoke of the problem of evil:

Evil is not merely a lack of something, but an effective agent, a living spiritual being, perverted and perverting. A terrible reality. Mysterious and frightening ... We know that this dark and disturbing spirit really exists and that he still acts with treacherous cunning; he is the secret enemy that sows errors and misfortunes in human history ... It is not a question of one Devil but of many ... This question of the Devil and the influence he can exert on individual persons as well as on communities, whole societies, and events, is a very important chapter of Catholic doctrine.[8]

The devil, then, has an important if obscure role in promoting evil in the world.

The problem of evil cannot be properly considered theologically apart from the principal elements of the Christian apocalyptic tradition, notably, the universal lordship of the risen Jesus and his power over evil.

The power of Jesus over the sea and the serpent

In both the Old and New Testaments, the natural images of the sea and of the serpent, images that have an apocalyptic tone, stand for evil in the world, all the evil that menaces us:

In the beginning God created the heavens and the earth. The earth was without form and void, and darkness was upon the face of the deep; and the Spirit of God was moving over the face of the waters (Gen. 1.1–2).

The book of Genesis pictures God as creating order out of chaos. The nothingness before creation is viewed as a formless and unordered void, a chaos. The image used is that of the sea: vast and formless waters, the symbol of total negativity, of nothingness, of non-existence. Although their neighbours, the Phoenicians, sent out fleets and saw the sea as opportunity, the people of Israel viewed the sea as containing the powers of evil, as standing for all that threatens human well-being: 'The Creator fixes the sea's limits, "shuts it in with doors"' (Job 38.8; see Gen. 1.10).

> Do you not fear me? says the Lord;
>> Do you not tremble before me?
> I placed the sand as the bound for the sea
>> a perpetual barrier which it cannot pass;
> though the waves toss, they cannot prevail,
>> though they roar, they cannot pass over it (Jer. 5.22).

The Creator reigns as Lord over even this dark and mysterious region, 'great and wide, teeming with creatures innumerable' (Ps. 104.25). He saves his people from the sea and this deliverance represents the salvation from all evil that God in his love and saving power wills for his own. The Lord says to Moses, ' "Lift up your rod and stretch out your hand over the sea and divide it, that the people of Israel may go on dry ground through the sea." . . . Thus the Lord saved Israel that day from the Egyptians' (Ex. 14.16, 30). 'He saved them for his name's sake, that he might make known his mighty power; he rebuked the Red Sea, and it became dry, and he led them through the deep as through a desert' (Ps. 106.8–9; see Isa. 11.15). God tells Joshua, 'The waters of the Jordan shall be stopped from flowing, and the waters flowing down from upstream shall be stopped in one heap' (Josh. 3.13). And so the psalmist sings, 'What ails you, O sea, that you flee? O Jordan, that you turn back?' (Ps. 114.5). The Lord saves Jonah from the whale's belly (Jonah 2.10). He saves Paul and his companions after their shipwreck (Acts 27.44), only one among three shipwrecks for Paul (II Cor. 11.25).

Jesus shows his lordship and his saving power by reigning over and pacifying the sea:

> And a great storm of wind arose, and the waves beat into the boat, so that the boat was already filling. But he was in the stern, asleep on the cushion; and they woke him and said to him, 'Teacher, do you not care if we perish?' And he awoke and rebuked the wind, and said to the sea, 'Peace! Be still!' And the wind ceased, and there was a great calm. He said to them, 'Why

43

are you afraid? Have you no faith?' And they were filled with awe, and said to one another, 'Who then is this, that even wind and sea obey him?' (Mark 4.37–41).[9]

Later, in high seas with a strong wind, Jesus walks on the water; when he gets into the boat, the wind ceases:

And when evening came, the boat was out on the sea, and he was alone on the land. And he saw that they were distressed in rowing, for the wind was against them. And about the fourth watch of the night he came to them, walking on the sea. He meant to pass them by, but when they saw him walking on the sea they thought it was a ghost, and cried out; for they all saw him, and were terrified. But immediately he spoke to them and said, 'Take heart, it is I; have no fear.' And he got into the boat with them, and the wind ceased. And they were utterly astounded (Mark 6.47–51).[10]

We can find in these two passages an implicit but clear reference to the credal account of creation in the book of Genesis. Just as the Creator dominated and ordered the chaotic sea 'in the beginning', so now Jesus dominates the sea and orders it to be still. There is reference, then, both to divine creative power and to divine saving power. In both texts, Jesus is revealed as possessing divine creative and saving power. The two 'sea' texts are epiphanies, accounts of Jesus revealed as divine and having divine power.[11] The sea here stands not only for nature-as-menacing, but for all the evils that beset us. Jesus' divine power to rescue his followers from nature-as-hostile represents his lordship over all creation and his power to save us from all evil.

'Walking on the sea' echoes the book of Job which says that 'God walked on the height of the strength of the sea' (Job 9).[12] God walks on the sea, in the book of Job, as on an opposing power or a defeated enemy. The book of Habbakuk has a similar passage: 'You trampled on the sea with your horse, a heap of many waters' (Hab. 3.15). God moves on the waters with a horse-drawn chariot, dominating the lawlessness and chaos of the sea, understood here as a force opposed to God. The complete dominance of the Creator over the sea, seen as opposing power, is brought out also by Psalm 77: 'When the waters saw you, they were afraid; yea, the deep trembled ... Your way was through the sea, your path through the great waters; yet your footprints were unseen' (Ps. 77.16–19). Jesus walks on the sea. He is Lord of creation and he dominates everything in creation that can harm us.

The point of the storm-stilling text, in which Jesus commands the wind and sea, and they obey him, is the same: the account is a revelation that Jesus has divine power to save his followers from distress.[13] Jesus not only calms the storm, but he rebukes his disciples: 'Why are you afraid? Have you no faith?' Why does Jesus rebuke men who stand in real danger, even in danger of death, for their fear? This rebuke can come only from one who, unthreatened by the storm, reigns over wind and sea. And so the prophet Nahum can say of God, 'He rebukes the sea' (Nahum 1.4). Jesus' words as well as his action in stilling the storm, reveal his lordship over creation and his power to save.

Before calming the storm, Jesus has revealed himself as both healer and exorcist; the calming of the storm shows him to be even more powerful than one who heals diseases and who casts out evil spirits; *even* wind and sea obey him. The rebuke to wind and sea parallels, in fact, what Jesus says during his first exorcism in Mark's gospel, 'But Jesus rebuked him [the unclean spirit], saying, "Be silent, and come out of him" ' (Mark 1.25); in stilling the storm, Jesus rebukes the wind and says to the sea, 'Peace! Be still!' (Mark 4.39). So the wind-and-sea calming stands in the same line as Jesus' exorcisms; it manifests his power over evil. But it manifests an even greater power than do the exorcisms: '*even* wind and sea obey him'.[14]

'He said to them, "Why are you afraid, O men of little faith?" ' (Matt. 8.26). In Matthew's gospel, just a little before the account of the calming of the storm, we find the parable of the builders. Whoever hears and does Jesus' words builds on rock and no storm can overcome it; whoever hears Jesus' words and does not do them builds on sand, 'and the rain fell, and the floods came, and the winds blew and beat against that house, and it fell' (Matt. 7.27).

Believing in Jesus and living out that faith protects us during storms. 'If it had not been for the Lord on our side . . . then the flood would have swept us away, the torrent would have gone over us; then over us would have gone the raging waters' (Ps. 124.1–5).

In the Old Testament, the dark and mysterious sea holds an even more frightening natural symbol of evil: the great serpent, named Rahab, or Leviathan. The great serpent appears in Mediterranean mythologies as the Creator's opponent; creation involves a cosmic struggle between Creator and the serpent or sea-monster or dragon. And it plays an important role in the extra-canonical Jewish apocalyptic literature. Even in the not strictly apocalyptic literature of the Old Testament, the great serpent appears as a more or less apocalyptic figure.[15]

God conquers the sea through his creative will, ruling it. So, too, he conquers the great serpent. 'By his power he stilled the sea; by his understanding he smote Rahab' (Job 26.12–13).[16] God catches Leviathan with a fish-hook and puts a rope in his nose (Job 41.1–2; see Job 3.8). 'The Lord with his great and strong sword will punish Leviathan the fleeing serpent, Leviathan the twisting serpent, and he will slay the dragon that is in the sea' (Isa. 27.1). The psalmist sings of the Lord's steadfast love and his faithfulness to the covenant with his people: 'You rule the raging of the sea; when its waves rise you still them; you crushed Rahab like a carcass' (Ps. 89.1–2, 9–10).

The great serpent remains, however, at least to some extent, an ambiguous figure in the Old Testament. 'The dragon that is in the sea' stands not only and always for evil. A few Old Testament texts find, in the terrible power of the serpent, a cause for wonder and awe at the power of God. At the end of the book of Job, Leviathan appears as the greatest of all God's creatures: 'upon the earth there is not his like' (Job 41.33). The very idea of Leviathan here crushes the man-centred conceit of Job, for the serpent is 'king over all the sons of pride' (Job 41.34). Psalm 104 sees Leviathan as God's great pet, created to play in the sea (Ps. 104.26), as does Job, chapter 41, which speaks of God's playing with Leviathan and even putting a leash on him (Job 41.5). Not merely a symbol of evil, the great serpent also acts as a manificent testimony to the terrible wisdom and power of God manifested in nature.

Note, however, that in Genesis 1.21, 'the great sea-monsters' are completely de-mythologized in accord with the priestly and de-sacralizing character of the document; they are seen simply as creatures, neither terrifying nor awe-inspiring. Psalm 148 even calls on the sea-monsters, along with the rest of nature, to praise the Lord! (Ps. 148.7).

Some texts in the Old Testament show quite clearly how closely the Hebrew mind associated God's act of creating the world and his triumph over the sea and over the great serpent. In the complex imagery of creation seen as conquest of the sea and the serpent, Israel understood God as both Creator and Deliverer, as both giving existence and saving from evil.

> Yet God, my king from the first,
> author of saving acts throughout the earth,
> by your power you split the sea in two,
> and smashed the heads of monsters on the waters.
> You crushed Leviathan's heads . . .
> You are master of day and night,
> you instituted light and sun,
> you fixed the boundaries of the world,
> you created summer and winter
>   (Ps. 74.14–17 Jerusalem Bible translation).[17]

The serpent, of course, symbolizes not only evil in general, but also that personal evil force we call Satan. The 'serpent deceived Eve by his cunning' (II Cor. 11.3),[18] and 'through the devil's envy death entered the world' (Wisd. 2.24; see I Tim. 2.14). Referring to God's promise that the serpent will be crushed under the feet of Eve's descendants, Paul, writing to the Romans, hopes that 'the God of peace will soon crush Satan under your feet' (Rom. 16.20, referring to Gen. 3). Satan appears again in serpent form in John's Apocalypse, as 'a great, red dragon' (Rev. 12.3), specifically named as the devil and Satan (Rev. 12.9; 20.2), 'that ancient serpent' (Rev. 20.2), who makes war on the church.

It is against this background that John's gospel speaks of Jesus lifted up on the cross. Jesus tells Nicodemus, 'As Moses lifted up the serpent in the wilderness, so must the Son of Man be lifted up, that whoever believes in him may have eternal life' (John 3.14–15). During the Exodus, 'the Lord sent fiery serpents among the people, and they bit the people' (Ex. 21.6). The people lamented to Moses, and he lamented to the Lord, who told Moses, ' "Make a fiery serpent and set it on a pole; and everyone who is bitten, when he sees it, shall live"; so Moses made a bronze serpent, and set it on a pole; and if a serpent bit anyone, he would look at the bronze serpent and live' (Ex. 21.8–9). It is not, however, the bronze serpent who heals those stricken with snake-bite, but rather the Lord, who shows in this way that it is he 'who delivers from every evil' (Wisd. 16.8). John's gospel proclaims the healing power of the cross by comparing Jesus on the cross with the bronze serpent that Moses raised up for the healing of the people of Israel in the desert. And so John quotes Zechariah, 'They shall look on him whom they have pierced' (John 19.37; Zech. 12.10).

In order to overcome sin and death and all evil, Jesus becomes sin, undergoes evil, dies. To conquer the serpent, Jesus becomes like the bronze serpent, lifted up so that we can look on him and be healed of the hurts that sin and other evils have inflicted on us. In this way, sharing in Jesus' death, our own deaths can become in him passages to glory. In Jesus' death, all death – the greatest defeat – lies defeated.

The meaning of the cross

What can the cross mean today with regard to our relationship with nature? The cross stands for victory over the lawlessness and iniquity involved in human misuse of nature and for the victory over whatever elements in nature threaten or menace us. The cross represents our share in Jesus' victory over sin, including our sinful use of nature. And it represents our victory, in Jesus, over that sum of all that threatens us in nature: death.

The cross of Jesus must be understood as a consequence of the incarnation and as leading to Jesus' resurrection. By the incarnation,

God, in Jesus, has joined himself in a new way to men and through men to the whole natural world. The relationship between God the Creator and the world, his creation, is fulfilled, brought to a head, in the incarnation. Jesus represents, and is, God-for-the-world, God involved in nature, God as part of his own creation. Far from indifferent to the world of nature, God, by the incarnation, has entered into a mutuality with it and with us by becoming human. God, infinitely free and self-sufficient by his own divine nature, has willed to need the world he made in order to complete the divine plan hidden from the ages but revealed in Christ.

Furthermore, Jesus, in his public life and in a special way in his passion and crucifixion, lived out fully the implications of his incarnation, taking the form of a servant, even to the point of death on the cross. Far from clinging to his dignity as God, he lived totally his humanity, refusing all offers and temptations to worldly power and glory, identifying himself not only with the prophet Daniel's messianic and triumphant image of the Son of Man who will come on the clouds of heaven but also with Isaiah's suffering servant who gives his life as a ransom for many. Jesus' involvement in the world took the form of service – of service to the Father through obedience and of service to the world by securing its salvation. This is why God raised him up to be the key-stone of all reality.

God pre-ordained Jesus from the beginning to be, risen, the future focal point of the world's movement, the goal of all history and true progress. But, in order to be that in his risen life, in order to be the central element of the world, Jesus first had to enter the world through being born, living, and dying on the cross. He descended, through his death, to the heart of the world so that, risen, he could act as the heart of the world.

By his death on the cross, Jesus reconciled everyone and all of nature in himself to the Father. But this reconciliation, accomplished in principle on the cross, works itself out gradually in history towards the end of time, when all things will find their definitive reconciliation in Jesus, Jesus will turn the kingdom over to the Father and God will be all in all.

Understood in this way, the cross of Jesus appears as the symbol and the reality not only of reparation and expiation for sin, but primarily as the symbol and the reality of progress through struggle and suffering and difficult labour. Jesus' death was, in the deepest sense, not a failure but a victory over the powers of darkness, a conquest of sin and death and all that oppresses us, a raising up of the world.

Teilhard de Chardin writes that the cross is 'the symbol not merely of the dark and retrogressive side of the universe in genesis, but also, and even more, of its triumphant and luminous side'. It is 'the symbol of progress and victory won through mistakes, disappointments, and hard work'. And it is the cross that we can 'offer to the worship of a world that has become conscious of what it was yesterday and what it awaits tomorrow'.[19]

This view of the cross emphasizes its orientation to Jesus' resurrection and so to the ultimate future that begins in an anticipatory way with the resurrection of Jesus. A positive understanding of the central act of our redemption stresses the forward and horizontal component of the cross, its relation to history not as a simply historical event but as that event that orders history in the direction of the world to come at history's termination. But it does not at all detract from the vertical or transcendent component of the cross. Jesus' death remains obedience to the Father's will, a total sacrifice of love to God, the action in which the world opens out to the transcendence of God and so to its own salvation. The 'forward' component of the cross, its future-directedness, and the 'upward' component, its relation to God in his transcendence, are brought into synthesis. The God of the 'upward' is the God of the 'forward'. The transcendent God has become, in Jesus, immanent in the world. And Jesus, having died, risen and taken his place at the right hand of the Father and as the goal of history, centres the world and its movement into the future on himself. Jesus is the God of both the 'upward' and the 'forward'; in him the 'horizontal' and the 'vertical' meet in synthesis.

The Christian doctrine of the cross does not deny the value of our involvement in the natural world as to-be-built towards a better future. On the contrary, the cross affirms that value and gives it its deepest meaning. All of us are called to be disciples of Jesus, to take up our crosses and to follow him. We are called by God to enter fully into the world, as Jesus did, to 'descend into' history, to become involved in constructing the kingdom. God does not ask us 'to swoon in the shadow, but to climb in the light, of the cross'.[20]

We are called, then, to take responsibility for our own lives, for nature, for the future. This responsibility is to be carried out in a sinful world, by taking up the cross of the struggle against the powers of darkness, against all that keeps us down. The cross stands for the struggle against evil, against all that oppresses us.

The sum of all evils, the summation of all that oppresses us, is death. This is why all simply human values, however valid and noble, finally fail: they cannot point to anything beyond death. They find defeat in the end because they end with death. This holds true not just for personal, individual values but also for social values, for the ethical systems of human collectivities, of democratic, capitalist, socialist, fascist and communist societies. They cannot lead man to ultimate victory, to life beyond death.

The strength of Christian values lies in the saving power of the cross of Christ which represents and which is the triumph over the last enemy and the greatest, death. By his death on the cross, Jesus has converted death into a passage to eternal life. Death has been conquered by being transformed into the way to resurrection. Insofar as anyone's death participates in the death of Jesus, takes place in union with him, that death shares in the victory of Jesus' death and leads to eternal salvation. In death, personal existence breaks up completely; death breaks and fragments the personal unity that has been built up during a lifetime. This final and total fragmentation is the necessary condition of the final personal synthesis in which God in Jesus puts the person back together, this time with a new and eternal wholeness, in glory.

At the end of history, the world, too, and all mankind, will die, break completely into fragments, so that God can rebuild it, transformed into the world to come. Everything of value that we have done or built or endured on earth will be found transformed and purified, burnished, after the world's death and rebirth.

In the same way, life can be, in Christ, a continuous dying and rising in Christ, a sharing in the paschal mystery. Each cross breaks up the provisory unity of the person, fragments the individual so that – to the extent that the cross is suffered and carried in union with Christ – God can put the pieces back together, this time in a higher synthesis in which the person finds a closer union with God. This is the path of personal spiritual progress.

The church, too, and every society insofar as it exists in Christ, follows the way of the cross. It lives, suffers and progresses, moving ahead through the pain of growth, coming apart and then coming together again closer to God. Suffering is, in this world, the price of progress. Each person, every society and mankind as a whole, is called to act out in history the life, death and resurrection of Jesus, sharing in those mysteries on the way to the final reconciliation of all things in the risen Christ.

The cross as revelation and salvation

In the cross of Jesus, iniquity (lawlessness, *anomie*) stands revealed for what it is, because the cross represents Jesus' obedience to God's law. Furthermore, every Christian who takes up his cross and follows Jesus gives witness to God's law by obeying it, by sharing in the obedience, in the cross of Jesus.

But the cross is more than revelation; it does more than witness to God's law by obedience. The cross is power. 'For the word of the cross is folly to those who are perishing, but to us who are being saved it is the power of God' (I Cor. 1.18). By his death on the cross, Jesus really did conquer evil. And every Christian who shares Jesus' cross shares in that victory over 'the mystery of lawlessness' (II Thess. 2.7).

IV

Golden Calves and Golden Tables: The Artist as Model for Transforming Nature

We live in and with nature. We form a part of nature. We work with and transform nature. Technology transforms nature, whether simple technology like primitive farming, or advanced technology like genetic engineering or building bridges. And art transforms nature. This chapter considers the artist as a kind of creator, a creative transformer of nature. Not simply that the artist – the painter, the sculptor, the composer, the musician or singer, the writer, the actor – takes more or less natural materials and transforms them into something higher. The artist creates in a more profound sense, transforms nature in a much deeper way.

The artist transforms nature by giving nature a new material interpretation. He interprets nature and in so doing transforms it, raises it to a higher level, recreates it.

The chapter concludes by pointing out that, in an extended sense, we are all artists. Nature is transformed in and through our lives. Our art is life itself, living. So the artist can act for us as a model.

Charisms

The classical muses who inspire the artist prefigure the Holy Spirit who truly inspires the Christian artist. The active capacity to be inspired by God in a particular way is a special gift called a charism.

There would seem to be, then, charisms of the arts.

What are charisms? The word 'charism' (from the Greek *charisma*, meaning gift) appears frequently in the Pauline writings. Sometimes it means simply a gift of grace, an effect or concretization of grace.[1] At other times, charism has the meaning that today's use gives it: a special gift, given to some but not to all, for the building up of the body of Christ that is the church. In this sense, a charism is a call to build up the community through some useful function and, at the same time, the means to fulfil that call. No one person has all the charisms, but the body of Christ possesses them all, distributed among the members of the body (I Cor. 12.7). And the greatest charisms are those that are most efficacious for building up the community. A charism, then, is a gift for service of some kind. Also, a charism is a new way, a special way, of relating to the Lord. It is a call to service (with the power to perform that service) and, also, a new way of being in relation to the Lord precisely in terms of that particular charism.

What are some charisms? The most commonly cited list is that of I Corinthians 12.8–10:

> For to one is given through the Spirit a word of wisdom, and to another, according to the same Spirit, a word of knowledge; to another, faith by the same Spirit, and to another gifts of healings by the one Spirit, to another the working of miracles, to another prophecy, to another the discernment of spirits, to another different kinds of tongues, and to another the interpretation of tongues, and in all these things operates the one and the same Spirit.

This list, of course, is far from exhaustive. Other lists of charisms can be found in the same chapter (12.28–30) and in the two succeeding chapters (13.1–3; 14.6; 14.26), as well as in Romans (12.6–8) and Ephesians (4.11). There is no complete list, and all the lists together do not seem to be complete. Some other charisms besides the ones mentioned in the list given above are: the gift of teaching, the gift of

54

assisting, the gift of governing and the gifts of almsgiving, ministry, exhorting, sharing, leadership, cheerfulness, evangelization, 'shepherding'. There is much overlapping in the various designated charisms and a few are obscure as to their meaning. What they have in common is that they are all special gifts of the Spirit, even if some charisms have natural gifts as correlates (e.g., leadership, teaching, cheerfulness) and may be built upon natural inclinations. In these charisms, the Holy Spirit becomes, we might say, almost visible, audible, tangible; all the charisms manifest the one Spirit whose gifts they are.

Charisms have always been a part of the Christian tradition in one way or another. Every age has had its gifted teachers, its great religious leaders, its miracle-workers. The founding and rapid spread of the Franciscans marked a great outpouring of the charism of evangelical poverty. There have always been those with the charism of missionary work (see Vatican II's document on the missions, *Ad gentes*, chapter IV, number 23) and there have always been many with the charism of consecrated celibacy (see I Cor. 7.7: 'I wish that all could be as I am, but each person has his own charism').

Charisms are referred to fourteen times by the Second Vatican Council, years before there was a Catholic charismatic renewal. The most important passage is from the Dogmatic Constitution on the Church:

It is not only through the sacraments and church ministries that the same Holy Spirit sanctifies and leads the People of God and enriches it with virtues. Allotting his gifts 'to everyone according as he wills' (I Cor. 12.11), he distributes special graces among the faithful of every rank. By these gifts he makes them fit and ready to undertake the various tasks or offices advantageous for the renewal and upbuilding of the church, according to the words of the Apostle: 'The manifestation of the Spirit is given to everyone for profit' (I Cor. 12.7). These charismatic gifts, whether they be the most outstanding or the more simple and widely diffused, are to be received with thanksgiving and consolation for they are exceedingly suitable and useful for the needs of the church.[2]

In the Eastern tradition of sacred art, the painting of icons has always been held a special gift, a particular grace, given to a few as a privileged way of relating to God and of serving the church. In other words, icon-painting is a charism.[3]

The painting of icons has always been rigidly controlled in the Eastern Christian tradition. The icon-painter must pray and fast and follow strict canons of painting. However, the painting of icons has never been used as an instrument of any ideology. This is how the icon tradition differs from contemporary Russian and Chinese Communist art. Art at the service of an ideology, instrumentalized art, becomes, always, non-art. This, I believe, is because the ideological instrumentalization of art closes it off to the transcendent, to God; and so, no longer open to an infinite horizon, closed up, it becomes something other than art. In a Kafka-esque metamorphosis, Communist art becomes propaganda. To a lesser extent, the Western Christian art tradition since Fra Angelico has had this closed quality because it has so often been instrumentalized, not by a political ideology, but by a moralizing ideology that has used art to 'edify' and to inculcate proper moral attitudes and spiritual sentiments.[4]

Icons, on the other hand, are not only religious art; they are *sacred* art – not art at the service of religion, but art at the service of God, art that opens out to an infinite horizon, that has a transcendental quality. An icon is a 'painting' only in the sense that the Bible is a 'book'. Icons transcend the category of 'paintings'. They are divine revelation, inherent in Christianity, which is not only the revelation of God's word but also of his image revealed in Jesus Christ. According to the Eastern Christian tradition, icons are on a level with the Bible, to be venerated.[5] They are inspired by the Holy Spirit, executed by special grace, painted 'in the Spirit' and according to a charism. Therefore they have a sacramental effect; they tend to 'give the grace they stand for', to lead the viewer to prayerful union with the subject (Christ, Mary, saints) represented by the icon. The icon, in fact, shares in the force and the glory of the person or persons that it represents. The power of God in a saint's life, for example, is actively present in the saint's icon, just as in his relics; this is why so many miracles have been attributed to icons.

But do the general theological principles of the icon tradition apply to all areas of art? Or do they apply only to art that has a specifically religious aim? My own opinion is that, for the Christian, all art is in some way sacred, because all art can be guided by grace and according to its proper charism. The Christian artist is called to pray, to fast and to work according to grace, according to the Holy Spirit, using the charism proper to that artist's art. (So there exist in the Orthodox Church iconographic saints, canonized for their art.) There must exist charisms of music, of sculpture, of painting, of architecture, of poetry, of drama and so on. They can be sought – that is, prayed for in faith. Just as a teacher can and should pray for the charism of teaching, and a leader for the charism of leadership, so too an artist ought to pray for the charism proper to that artist's particular art. The idea of charisms of art is not new:

> And Moses said to the people of Israel: 'See, the Lord has called by name Bezalel the son of Uri, son of Hur, and he has filled him with the Spirit of God, with ability, with intelligence, with knowledge, and with all craftsmanship, to devise artistic designs, to work in gold and silver and bronze, in cutting stones for setting, and in carving wood, for work in every skilled craft (Ex. 35. 30–33).

The possibility of some form of idolatry always exists. It seems to me that any art not open to the transcendent and to being 'graced', inspired by the Holy Spirit, risks being instrumentalized by some earthly 'religion' (communism, pornography, business and others) or – perhaps worse – becoming an end in itself. Either way, it falls into idolatry. In the war between Abijah, King of Judah, who was faithful to God, and Jeroboam, King of Israel, who had brought in pagan practices and idolatry, Abijah cries out to the troops of Jeroboam:

> And now you think to withstand the kingdom of the Lord in the hands of the sons of David because you are a great multitude and

have with you the golden calves which Jeroboam made you for gods. Have you not driven out the priests of the Lord and made priests for yourselves like the peoples of other lands? . . . But as for us, the Lord is our God, and we have not forsaken him. We have priests ministering to the Lord who are sons of Aaron, and Levites for their service. They offer to the Lord every morning and every evening burnt offerings and incense of sweet spices, set out the show bread on the table of pure gold, and care for the golden lampstand that its lamps may burn every evening (II Chron. 13.8–11).

As far as art goes, the opposition is between art at the service of 'religion' and art at the service of God, between idolatry and sacrifice, between the golden calf and the golden table. Art done 'in the Spirit' gives praise to God, gives him glory, is, somehow, 'sacrifice'.

Art as charismatic revelation

In Western civilization, religious art has almost always aimed at edification, at evoking sentiments of piety, at directing the imagination toward reverence and prayer. The icon, on the other hand, reveals God. And, in this theophany, the icon brings the viewer into communion with the divine sphere, with Jesus Christ or the Trinity or whatever saints are represented in the icon. What is true of the icon is true of any art done according to the Holy Spirit. Inspired art inspires, can be the vehicle or the instrument of revelation. More, inspired art is revelation.

The theology of revelation tells us that all creation and all history in some way reveal God to us. God's creative word, spoken in the beginning, reveals the Creator in its effects. God speaks ('Let there be light') and things exist. Existing, they reveal their Creator. The inspired artist interprets reality seen as revelation. He is the exegete of creation; and his art is its hermeneutics. God's word is revealed in his creation and the artist brings that word to further expression, interpreting and formulating it in some kind of human language.

In the effect of every charism, because that effect is inspired by the

Holy Spirit, the Spirit becomes – so to speak – 'tangible', 'visible', 'audible'. The charism of art, then, makes grace visible, reveals God in the concrete. In this way, the artist co-creates with the Creator, re-creating according to the Spirit, in art, God's creation. And, as does God's own creation, the artist's creation reveals the divine.

Art as revelation has an apocalyptic dimension. The Spirit that inspires art is the eschatological Spirit, the Holy Spirit who breaks through into the present from God's promised future. The kingdom of God is to come and yet it is here already, breaking in on us through the Holy Spirit as the pledge of future glory and making all things new now. The Holy Spirit renews us towards the future. Partly, the Spirit renews through inspired art. Art makes new creations, makes things new by creating new things. Art formulates God's future breaking into the present by making symbols of the future. Art brings the future to expression now.

Art as charismatic service

Every charism is both a special way of relating to God and, at the same time, for service, for building up the community, for the common good (I Cor. 12.7). Charisms of art, also, are for serving. This service, since it is Christian service, takes place in love; and it has the shape of the cross.

God not only creates, but has entered fully into his creation. The creative word of the Father has become flesh and dwelt among us. So, too, the artist 'descends into' the work of art, puts the artist's self into it, becomes in some way incarnate in what is created. The artist participates in the mystery of God's continuous creation; and also, by going out of himself, by emptying himself into what is created, the artist enters into the pattern of the incarnation.

In entering into what is created, every creator (Creator) lays himself on the line, risks himself, is *in* his creation – which becomes in some sense himself. A mother's child is her other self. A teacher's subject is, in some sense, the teacher's self; a painter paints himself; an actor's *persona*, mask, role, refracts, not hides, the self-given-in-acting.

The artist goes out of the artist's self, falls into the ground to bear fruit, dies, is somehow, like St Paul, crucified with his Creator. An artist lives on the edge, always dying and rising. Again, the pattern is that of the incarnation and, going further, of the death and resurrection of Jesus (see Phil. 2.6–11).

Christian art and Christian life

By analogy we can speak of Christian living as an art, although living goes far beyond being an art. The Christian, then, is a kind of artist of life in the daily activity of transforming nature through everyday work and relationships. Like the artist in art, the Christian in life can be tempted to idolatry, to making labour a golden calf rather than a golden table, an idol rather than a sacrificial action that goes beyond itself and refers to the Lord as service performed for him, according to his will.

Further, what the Christian does, like what the artist does, can be 'revelation', can witness to the Lord, can reveal God to others through how the Christian lives and works. In our service, too, we imitate the artist, entering into what we do, risking ourselves, putting ourselves *into* what we do. And so, like the artist, we die to ourselves, as the seed in the parable falls into the ground to bear fruit. We live on the edge, always dying and rising again in the pattern of the mystery of the death and resurrection of Jesus.

Again by analogy, if Christian living is like an art, what might be the charism proper in Christian life? And again, it goes far beyond being a charism; it is a whole *way* of living. St Paul, after his discussion of charisms in I Corinthians, chapter 12, writes: 'And I will show you a still more excellent way' (I Cor. 12.31). He goes on to describe love. Love is the life of every charism and without love every charism is nothing – 'a noisy gong, a clanging cymbal' (I Cor. 13.1). Christian life is an art and its charism is love.

At the same time, Christian life without the arts is not truly Christian. Art celebrates with God our salvation, expresses God's Holy Spirit in our lives, speaks the gladness that grace gives us. The

Father welcomes back all his prodigal children and so no wonder that, as the elder son comes in from the field to his father's house, he hears 'music and dancing' (Luke 15.25).

V

Down to the Garden: Finding God in Nature

> I went down to the nut garden,
>   to look at the blossoms of the valley,
> to see whether the vines had budded,
>   whether the pomegranates were in bloom.
> Before I was aware, my imagination put me
>   in a chariot beside my prince
>   (Song of Solomon 6.11–12).

Like the maiden in the Song of Songs, I can go down to the nut garden, to look at the vines and the flowers; and I can find myself, transported in my mind, beside the prince. Rather than give to this text a literal interpretation like most modern exegetes, and rather than follow the allegorical interpretation (the maiden is Israel or the church, the prince is God) of the writers of the church's first four centuries, we can emulate St John of the Cross and other spiritual writers in understanding it as a metaphor of our relationship in the world with God.[1] And so we might say: the garden is nature, the prince is God and each of us is the maiden. Like the maiden, let us go down to the garden.

There are six basic ways of finding God in nature: through service, through praise, through thanksgiving, through contemplation, through meditation and by seeing nature as a metaphor for Jesus Christ in his humanity. We can take them one at a time.

The Second Vatican Council's Pastoral Constitution on the Church in the Modern World *(Gaudium et spes)* takes an eschatological view of nature, sees it as oriented through us not simply to the Lord but to the Lord-who-comes and to the world to come.

> For after we have nurtured on earth all the good things of nature and the fruits of our own labour, in the Spirit of the Lord and according to his mandate, we will find them again, purified of every stain, burnished and transfigured, when Christ hands over to the Father a kingdom eternal and universal, . . . a kingdom already present in mystery.[2]

Working with nature, transforming it, we not only obey the Lord in exercising our dominion over nature, but we build towards the world to come. We build the remote material, so to speak, of the New Jerusalem. The Lord intends that nothing we do or build here in this world be lost; we will find all the positive aspects of even our most humble labours 'burnished and transfigured' in some mysterious way in the world to come, in the ultimate future of glory with the Lord.

The document states that mankind has extended its mastery over nearly the whole of nature, and continues to do.[3] And it goes on to say that this activity accords with God's will:

> Created in God's image, we have received a mandate to subject to ourselves the earth and all that it contains, and to govern the world with justice and holiness; a mandate to relate ourselves and the totality of things to him who was to be acknowledged as the Lord and Creator of all. Thus, by the subject of all things, the name of God would be wonderful in all the earth. This mandate concerns even the most ordinary everyday activities. Men and women . . . can justly consider that by their labour they are unfolding the Creator's work.[4]

Our work in transforming nature in no way 'competes with' God or somehow challenges him; that work 'is a flowering of God's own mysterious design'.[5] In fact, Christianity calls us, binds us, to serve the Lord and our brothers and sisters by transforming nature.[6] Nature is a garden. The transformation of nature calls for service that involves not only work but sometimes suffering. Working in the garden has the form of taking up the cross and following Jesus. Jesus suffered, sweated bloody sweat, was in agony in the garden. Christian service takes the shape of the cross. Service toward the transformation of nature is cruciform.

The result of the human history of the sinful use of nature is our alienation from nature. Sin causes nature to turn against us; the garden of Eden changed drastically after the sin of Adam and Eve. In exploiting nature as if it were a mine instead of tending it like the garden it is, we have misused nature. We redeem it, overcoming our alienation from it, by working with it, by tending the garden. And this redemptive service of transforming nature is in the structure of the cross.

Further, serving the Lord now by transforming nature calls for service in the economic, social and political orders. For nature does not lead some isolated existence; in this age, we find nature politicized, economically exploited, having social results. Serving the Lord, then, necessarily involves action for social and economic justice and so for a more just political order to bring about justice.

Relating to the Lord through nature by means of responsible service, we give him glory through nature; our service becomes a kind of praise.

Praise

Or we can praise God directly through and for the wonders and beauties of nature that he has given us, referring them directly back to him for his own sake, because he is the kind of God that has created these things. A *leitmotif* of the sixteenth and seventeenth centuries was that we are created to give God glory through both service and praise.

Saint Ignatius Loyola, in his *Spiritual Exercises*, begins the 'First Principle and Foundation' of the *Exercises*, a kind of meditative prologue, by saying that we have been 'created to praise, reverence, and serve God our Lord'; he frequently speaks of our call to the 'service and praise' of Jesus Christ. Ignatius Loyola understands service and praise as gifts from the Lord, as the activities we were created for, and as our response to the Lord's personal call. His *Exercises* call us to *greater* service and praise, to serve and praise the Lord better. Francis de Sales, Leonard Lessius and many of the Reformation theologians teach the same doctrine.

Later, the First Vatican Council (1869–70) solemnly declared that 'the world was made for the glory of God'.[7] This must be understood according to the theology of that time; the 'glory of God' includes both the glory that God gives to his creatures and by which they manifest his greatness and also the praise (glory) we should give God for the manifestations, in nature for example, of his greatness. In the nineteenth and early twentieth centuries, these romantic ideas were central in Christian writing and art. Nature shows forth God's glory. 'The world is charged with the grandeur of God; it will flame out like shining from shook foil', wrote Gerard Manley Hopkins in his poem 'God's Grandeur'. And we are called to lift up praise to God, to glorify him in response to his glory that he reveals to us. Elizabeth of the Trinity wanted to be nothing other than 'a praise of glory';[8] 'glory be to God', Hopkins wrote, '. . . praise him'.[9]

If the twentieth century has left much of nineteenth-century romanticism behind, this should not blind us to the truth of our call to praise God in and through and for nature, nor should it deprive us of the joy of using the God-given gift of praising the Lord for nature, the work of his hands.

What is praise? Praise is not the same as, for example, thanksgiving. When I thank God, I show him my gratitude for his gifts and I attribute these to him in my thanksgiving; but when I praise God, I give him credit, so to speak, not for his gifts, but for himself. Praise is the point at which thanksgiving becomes thanksgiving to God for being God, as in the words of the *Gloria*, '. . . we give you thanks . . . for your glory'. I can praise God for himself and for his qualities – his goodness, love, wisdom, and infinite greatness. I can also praise him for his actions, for his creation – beginning with his creation of nature. I do not exactly thank him, but rather I praise him for nature, because it is the Lord who has created nature and who is Lord over it.

Praise is similar to adoration, but praise is more active and extrovert; it speaks interiorly or out loud, shouting, singing, dancing. Praise celebrates God. Adoration implies silent prostration before God,[10] whereas praise is voiced:

And from the throne came a voice crying,
  'Praise our God, all you his servants,
    you who fear him, small and great.'
Then I heard what seemed to be the voice of a great multitude,
like the sound of many waters and like the sound of mighty
thunder-peals, crying,
  'Hallelujah! For the Lord our God
    the Almighty reigns.
  Let us rejoice and exult and give
    him the glory' (Rev. 19.5–7).

Praise simply acclaims and applauds God. It does not look to the past, as thanksgiving does, nor to the future, as prayer of petition does; it looks straight at the Lord and claps its hands.

A number of the Psalms are prayers or hymns of praise of God for nature. For example, Psalm 104 praises the Lord for his creation:

You set the earth on its foundations,
  so that it should never be shaken.
You covered it with the deep as with a garment;
  the waters stood above the mountains.
At your rebuke they fled;
  at the sound of your thunder they took to flight.
The mountains rose, the valleys sank down
  to the place which you appointed for them (Ps. 104.5–8).

It then goes on to praise God for the various things of the earth.

Some Psalms invite nature itself to praise God. 'Make a joyful noise to the Lord, all the earth.'[11] 'Sing to the Lord, all the earth' (Ps. 96.1).

Praise him, sun and moon,
  praise him all you shining stars!
Praise him you highest heavens,
  and you waters above the heavens . . .
Praise the Lord from the earth,
  you sea monsters and all deeps,
fire and hail, snow and frost,
  stormy wind fulfilling his command!
Mountains and all hills,
  fruit trees and all cedars!
Beasts and all cattle,
  creeping things and flying birds! . . .
Let them praise the name of the Lord (Ps. 148.3–4, 7–10, 13).

So nature itself praises God: 'Let the heavens praise your wonders,
O Lord' (Ps. 89.5); 'All the earth worships you; they sing praise to
your name' (Ps. 66.4).

Other psalms praise God for his attributes manifested in nature.
Psalm 147 praises him for his goodness and providence: 'Make
melody on the lyre to our God! He covers the heavens with clouds,
he prepares rain for the earth, he makes grass grow upon the hills,
he gives to the beasts their food' (Ps. 147.7–9). Psalm 89 praises the
Lord for his fidelity and governance in power: 'I will sing of your
steadfast love, O Lord, for ever . . . You rule the raging of the sea;
when its waves rise, you still them' (Ps. 89.1, 9). And Psalm 136
gives praise to God because of his covenant love for and faithfulness
to what he has made:

O give thanks to the Lord, for he is good,
  for his steadfast love endures for ever . . .
O give thanks . . .
to him who made the great lights,
  for his steadfast love endures for ever;
the sun to rule over the day,
  for his steadfast love endures for ever;
the moon and stars to rule over the night,
  for his steadfast love endures for ever . . . (Ps. 136.1–9).

Ignatius Loyola ends his book of *Spiritual Exercises* with the 'Contemplation for Obtaining Love'. He directs the person making the *Exercises* to consider, first, God's gifts to him, such as the gifts of nature, one by one,

> . . . pondering with great affection how much God our Lord has done for me, and how much he has given me of what he possesses, and finally, how much as far as he can, the same Lord desires to give himself to me according to his divine decrees.[12]

A second point is to consider how God dwells in nature, giving it existence, giving plants their life, giving animals feeling, giving us being and life and feeling and intelligence since we are created in his image.

A third point in the 'Contemplation' considers,

> . . . how God works and labours for me in all creatures upon the face of the earth; that is, he conducts himself as one who labours. Thus, in the heavens, the elements, the plants, the fruits, the cattle, etc., he gives being, confers life and sensation, etc.[13]

The fourth and final point,

> . . . is to consider all blessings and gifts as descending from above . . . as the rays of light descend from the sun, and as the waters flow from their fountains.[14]

The 'Contemplation for Obtaining Love' is a way of looking at all creation, and at nature in particular, with gratitude to the Creator for his gifts. Why is it called a contemplation 'for obtaining love'? Because of its dynamic, because of how it functions. It leads me to contemplate God's gifts in nature, to find him in those gifts, to see him as giving me his gifts and – through his gifts – himself. It leads me to realize more deeply, to interiorize more, the fact that God loves me personally. I know, because he gives me his gifts. And this inspires gratitude in me and thanksgiving to the Giver for his gifts, for himself, for his love. And so I am led to a greater love for God; I 'obtain' greater love for the Lord.

These three ways of finding God in nature – through service, praise and thanksgiving – come together when we take part in the Lord's Supper, the Eucharist. The Eucharist celebrates our service towards the transformation of nature in the prayers of offering the bread and wine. We bless the God of all creation, because through his goodness 'we have this bread to offer, which earth has given and human hands have made', and because 'we have this wine to offer, fruit of the vine and work of human hands'. Further, the Eucharist celebrates God's transformation by his Holy Spirit of our efforts to transform nature – at the consecration, when the 'work of human hands' becomes the body and blood of Jesus.

Praise runs all through the celebration of the Eucharist. In the preface to the fourth eucharistic prayer, we praise the Creator 'in the name of every creature under heaven'. Preface number five for Sundays praises God because he has made all things, because all times and seasons obey his laws, because he has created us in his own image and set us over the whole of nature in all its wonder. It praises God because he has made us stewards of nature to praise him day by day for the marvels of his wisdom and power. The fourth eucharistic prayer praises God because he has formed us in his likeness, set us over all nature to serve him, our Creator, and to rule over all creatures.

And of course the whole eucharistic celebration is a prayer of thanksgiving; 'eucharist' means 'thanksgiving'. All of nature, repre-sented by the bread and wine (nature transformed) is offered to the Father, then changed into his Son, Jesus, to be offered anew. The Eucharist gives us the best model for thanking the Father for nature. We refer it back to him, with loving thankfulness, through and with and in his Son and our Saviour, Jesus. 'Through him, with him, in him, in the unity of the Holy Spirit, all glory and honour is yours, Almighty Father, forever and ever. Amen.'

Contemplating God through nature

Psalm 104 looks at the Creator, contemplates him, through nature. In nature, the psalmist sees glorified: God's wisdom, in the governance of nature; his goodness, in providing for all his creatures; his power in that he has as a toy the great serpent itself. The psalmist admires nature and, through nature, its Creator, recognized in the nature he has created and takes care of:

Bless the Lord, O my soul!
O Lord, my God, you are very great!
You are clothed with honour and majesty,
    you cover yourself with light as with a garment . . .
You make the clouds your chariot,
    you ride on the wings of the wind . . .
You make springs gush forth in the valleys;
    they flow between the hills,
    they give drink to every beast of the field, . . .
From your lofty abode, you water the mountains;
    the earth is satisfied with the fruit of your work . . .
Lord, how manifold are your works!
In wisdom you have made them all;
    the earth is full of your creatures.
There is the sea, great and wide,
    teeming with creatures innumerable,
    living things both small and great.
There go the ships,
    and Leviathan whom you formed to play in it.
They all look to you
    to give them their food in due season . . .
When you send forth your Spirit,
    they are created;
And you renew the face of the earth . . .
I will sing to the Lord as long as I live;
I will sing praise to my God while I have being . . .
Bless the Lord, O my soul!
Praise the Lord!

The psalm moves from an initial burst of praise to the contempla-tion of God through nature and in it, and ends with another burst of praise.

Job's contemplation, in chapters 38 to 41, begins rather in misery and dejection and even a certain resentment towards God, moves to the contemplation of God in the wonders of his creation, and sees there the Creator's transcendent wisdom that goes way beyond what we can comprehend. Contemplation of the Lord in and through nature ends in humility. 'I had heard of you by hearsay,' Job tells God, 'but now my eye sees you; therefore I humble myself and repent in dust and ashes' (Job 42.5–6).

Ben Sirach, in the book of Wisdom, has a long poem of the contemplation of God through nature (Ecclus. (Ben Sira) 42.15–43, 33), beginning with sun, moon and stars and working down to the wonders of nature on the earth. The poem begins in a didactic way, contemplates God in nature, and ends in an exhortation to praise and glorify the Creator.

In the letter to the Romans, Paul excoriates the pagans who failed to turn to God even though they saw him in the nature around them (Rom. 1.18, 32). Although they saw God in nature, they did not turn to him in love. And this is what contemplating God through nature is: a turning to him and a looking, with love for him, at his attributes, manifested in nature. Nature 'tells the glory of God' (Ps. 19.1).

Nature, we said at the beginning of this chapter, is a garden. The first person recorded to have seen Jesus after his resurrection was Mary Magdalene. She found him in the garden and recognized him there. The Lord invites us to recognize him in nature, in the garden, and to look at him, to contemplate him there.

Meditation on nature as leading to God

We can reflect on nature and so arrive at conclusions about God. Reflecting on what we see in nature, we can learn more about nature's Author.

He who planted the ear, does he not hear?
He who formed the eye, does he not see? (Ps. 94.9).

A reflection on the greatness and majesty of the heavens leads to a greater appreciation of man's smallness and God's greatness (Ps. 8.3–9).

The presence of mystery in nature leads to a reflection that concludes to a greater understanding of the mysteriousness and incomprehensibility of God and of his ways. 'As you do not know the way of the wind, or how the bones grow in the womb, so you do not know the work of God who governs everything' (Eccles. 11.5). God's ways are above our ways. Similarly, a reflection on nature leads to a greater appreciation of the Lord's mercy:

> For as the heavens are high above the earth,
>   so great is his steadfast love towards those who fear him;
> as far as the east is from the west,
>   so far does he remove our transgressions from us
>   (Ps. 103. 11–12).[15]

And the enduringness of the hills and mountains helps us to consider the faithfulness of God's love:

> For the mountains may depart,
>   and the hills be removed,
> but my steadfast love shall not depart from you (Isa. 54.10).

We can learn about the Lord by meditating, considering, the nature he has created.

Nature as metaphor for the humanity of Christ

In his teaching, Jesus uses images from nature, especially from nature as found in the daily lives of the people to whom he speaks – images of fields, of the weather, of the sea, of water, of light, of birds and animals. He uses some of these images as metaphors for himself. 'I am the light of the world' (John 8.1). 'I am the true vine' (John 15.1). From the time of John the Baptist, the church has referred to Jesus as the Lamb of God. He is the Sun of Justice. He is prayed to as the Sacred Heart, identified with his own human heart as a natural symbol of his love.

Acting on this precedent, poets see metaphors for Jesus Christ in nature. Gerard Manley Hopkins, in his poem 'The Windhover', takes a flying falcon as a metaphor for Christ. The falcon, 'morning's minion, kingdom of daylight's dauphin', stirs the poet's heart and leads him to pray to Jesus Christ, in the poem's second verse. In Hopkins' poem, 'That Nature is a Heraclitean Fire and of the Comfort of the Resurrection', Jesus is an 'immortal diamond'. At my own resurrection,

> In a flash, at a trumpet's crash,
> I am all at once what Christ is
> since he was what I am, and
> This Jack, joke, poor potsherd, patch,
> matchwood, immortal diamond
> Is immortal diamond.[16]

For Francis Thompson, Jesus is the 'Hound of Heaven'. For John of the Cross, Jesus is:

> ... the mountains,
> The lonely wooded valleys,
> The strange islands,
> The noisy rivers,
> The whistling of winds in love.[17]

Thomas Merton, in his poem, 'The Vine', sees a vine on a hill near his monastery, barren during the winter and early spring and blossoming near Easter time, as a metaphor not only for Jesus as the true vine but also as a metaphor for the whole paschal mystery. And Joseph Mary Plunkett finds Jesus in the nature around him:

> I see his blood upon the rose
> And in the stars the glory of his eyes,
> His body gleams amid eternal snows,
> His tears fall from the skies.
>
> I see his face in every flower;
> The thunder and the singing of the birds
> Are but his voice – and carven by his power
> Rocks are his written words.

All pathways by his feet are worn,
His strong heart stirs the ever-beating sea,
His crown of thorns is twined with every thorn,
His cross is every tree.[18]

Notes

Note to the Reader

1. For this reason, René Dubois recommends St Benedict rather than St Francis as the Christian model, since he considers the latter too passive in regard to nature; see his *A Theology of the Earth*, a lecture published in the form of a booklet by the Smithsonian Institution, Washington DC 1969, pp. 6–7. Cf. Kenneth R. Boulding, *The Meaning of the Twentieth Century – The Great Transition*, Harper, New York 1964, p. 6; regarding the Benedictines of the sixth century, Boulding writes that 'for almost the first time in history we had intellectuals who worked with their hands, and belonged to a religion which regarded the physical world as in some sense sacred and capable of enshrining goodness'.

2. Some of the material in this book has appeared previously: the second chapter in a different form in *The Spirit of God in Christian Life*, ed. E. Malatesta SJ, © 1977 by The Missionary Society of Saint Paul the Apostle in the State of New York (used by permission of Paulist Press); the fourth chapter in *Theological Renewal* XVI, 1980, pp. 27–32 (reproduced by permission).

I 'And God saw that it was good'

1. See also: Ps. 104; 74.12–27; 95.1–7; Eccles. 16.25–29; 42.15–43.34; Job 38, 39, 40, 42; Amos 4.13; 5.8–9; 9.5–6.

2. See Ps. 8.3–6; see also B. Anderson, 'Human Dominion over Nature', *Biblical Studies in Contemporary Thought*, ed. M. Ward, Greeno Hadden, Somerville, Mass. 1975, pp. 34–45, for a good comparison of Ps. 8 and Gen. 1.26–8.

3. See Vatican II's Pastoral Constitution on the Church in the Modern World, *Gaudium et spes*, nos. 33, 34, 39.

4. James Logan, 'The Secularization of Nature', *Christians and the Good*

Earth, Faith-Man-Nature Group, Alexandria, Va. 1968, p. 104; this is an excellent article. Cf. also Robert W. Platman, 'Theology and Ecology: A Problem for Religious Education', *Religious Education* LXVI, 1971, pp. 14–32.

5. I am following here the exegesis of H. Schlier, 'The Pauline Body-Concept', *The Church*, Kennedy, New York 1963, pp. 44–58.

6. Gianfranco Bussetto, 'Ecologia e religione', *Corriere della Sera*, 30 November 1978, p. 5.

7. Lynn White, 'The Historical Roots of Our Ecological Crisis', *Science* CLV, 1967, pp. 1203–1207.

8. Leo Marx, 'American Institutions and Ecological Ideals', *Science* CLXX, 1970, p. 948; Paul Ehrlich, *How to Be a Survivor*, Ballantine, New York 1971, p. 129.

9. Max Nicholson, *The Environmental Revolution*, Hodder 1969, p. 264.

10. See H. Paul Santmire, *Brother Earth: Nature, God, and Ecology in Time of Crisis*, Nelson, New York 1970; Joseph Sittler, *The Ecology of Faith*, Fortress, Philadephia 1970; Michael Hamilton, ed., *This Little Planet*, Scribner, New York 1970; Ian Barbour, ed., *Science and Secularity: The Ethics of Technology*, Harper, New York 1970; idem, ed., *That Earth Might Be Fair*, Harper, New York 1972; Christopher Derrick, *The Delicate Creation*, Devin-Adair, London 1972; John Passmore, *Man's Responsibility for Nature*, Duckworth 1974; Thomas S. Derr, *Ecology and Human Need*, Fortress, Philadelphia 1975; Don E. Marietta, Jr, 'Religious Models and Ecological Decision Making', *Zygon* XII, 1977, pp. 151–166; Hugh Montefiore, 'Man and Nature: A Theological Assessment', *Zygon* XII, 1977, pp. 199–211; Rowland Moss, 'God, Man, and Nature', *The Teilhard Review* XIII, 1978, pp. 89–103. Even more recently, Garrett Hardin has attacked the very idea of a caring God as at the root of bad Western ecological attitudes and practices. He understands the Christian concept of God to have so functioned historically as to deplete human will and initiative to prepare for the future. For Hardin, the enemy of responsible stewardship of nature is not a wrong or incomplete idea of Christian stewardship, but God understood as our Father. 'It is high time', he writes, 'that we try to reshape human beings into mature creatures who no longer depend on the support of a benevolent Providence under any name' ('Ecology and the Death of Providence', *Zygon* XV, 1980, p. 67). Hardin, then, sees Christianity itself as an enemy.

11. See the classic study of H. Richard Niebuhr, *Christ and Culture*, Harper, New York 1951, chapter 5, 'Christ and Culture in Paradox', pp.

149–189. Helmut Thielicke serves as a good example of a contemporary Lutheran theologian on the person-nature relationship. Operating out of a Lutheran conception of nature, Thielicke parallels Gen. 9.1–2 ('And God blessed Noah and his sons, and said to them, "Be fruitful and multiply, and fill the earth. The fear of you and the dread of you shall be upon every beast of the earth, and upon every bird of the air, upon everything that creeps on the ground and on all the fish of the sea; into your hand they are delivered" ') and Gen. 1.28 ('And God said to them, "Be fruitful and multiply, and fill the earth and subdue it; and have dominion over the fish of the sea and over the birds of the air and over every living thing that moves upon the earth" '). The differences in the two parallel texts indicate the radical change in nature after the fall. Fear, dread and terror hold a fallen and rebellious creation in check. Our dominion over nature now, after the fall, is one of power-to-be-exercised to inculcate terror and dread in nature. Our relationship with nature is not one of harmonious complementarity, but a relationship of master to unruly servant or slave. See: *Der Glaube der Christenheit*, 5th ed., Vandenhoeck & Ruprecht 1965, pp. 117–172; *Theologische Ethik*, vol. II, part 1, 2nd ed., Mohr, Tubingen 1959, pp. 655–666.

II 'All creation groans'

1. See G. Gutiérrez, *A Theology of Liberation*, SCM Press 1974. See also P. Berryman, 'Latin American Liberation Theology', *Theological Studies* XXXIV, 1973, pp. 357–395. One notable exception among contemporary theologians is Rosemary Radford Ruether, who does come to grips with our relationship with nature, emphasizing the social and political dimensions of that relationship; see the chapter on 'Ecology and Human Liberation: A Conflict between the Theology of History and the Theology of Nature?' in her book *To Change the World* (the Kuyper Lectures at the Free University in Amsterdam), SCM Press 1981, pp. 57–70.

2. J. Sittler, *Essays on Nature and Grace*, Fortress, Philadelphia 1972.

3. See, for example, articles by or about these theologians in *Process Theology: Basic Writings*, ed. E. Cousins, Newman, New York 1971.

4. See the often reprinted article of Lynn White, 'The Historical Roots of Our Ecological Crisis', *Science* CLV, 3767, 10th March 1967, pp. 1203–1207. See also the last part of chapter I of this book.

5. Little theological reflection has taken place with regard to dialectical relationships. See, however, the writings of Gaston Fessard, especially *De l'actualité historique*, vol. I, Desclée de Brouwer, Paris 1960. See also the

excellent synthesis of Fessard's ideas on dialectic by Edouard Pousset, 'Christian Man in Dialectic', *A Christian Anthropology*, Abbey Press, Indiana 1974, pp. 31–50. Fessard's dialectic is broadly Hegelian.

6. See, for example, E. A. Olssen, 'Marx and the Resurrection', *Journal of the History of Ideas* XXIX, 1968, pp. 131–140; G. Fessard, 'The Theological Structure of Marxist Atheism', *Concilium* VI, 2, 1966, pp. 5–13 (British edition). It should be noted that I do not use the word 'nature' in precisely the same sense that Marx does. Marx, it seems to me, uses the word always to mean all material reality.

7. See S. Lyonnet, 'The Redemption of the Universe', *The Church*, op. cit., pp. 136–156.

8. See P. Henriot, 'Social Sin and Conversion: A Theology of the Church's Social Involvement', *Chicago Studies* XI, 1972, pp. 3–18; 'Politics and the Priest', *Commonweal* XCVI, 1972, pp. 495–498; 'The Concept of Social Sin', distributed by the Institute of Human Relations, Loyola University, New Orleans. Latin-American theology of liberation has seen clearly the master-slave relationship between sinful social structures and oppressed peoples. It has, however, not sufficiently understood the relationships of complementarity between person and nature, and between the person and God-in-Jesus-Christ. Liberation theology, failing to consider adequately the strengthening function of the person-nature relationship and the properly liberating effect of the person-God relationship, has seen the problem (sinful social structures) but has only dimly perceived the solution (salvation by God). It has failed, also, to understand its often used paradigm of the exodus, not taking enough into account how Israel grew in strength precisely through working (in union with nature) in slavery and how Israel's liberation began with prayer ('then we cried out to the Lord' – Deut. 26.7) and came about through the power of God ('and the Lord brought us out of Egypt with a mighty hand and an outstretched arm' – Deut. 28.8). Part of the problem of Latin-American liberation theology comes not, as some have supposed, from taking Marxist categories too seriously, but from not taking the categories of Marxist dialectic seriously enough. The result has been a kind of neo-pelagianism.

9. Friedrich Engels said more than he knew when he called Christianity 'a great revolutionary movement' (see 'The Book of Revelation', *Marx and Engels on Religion*, Schocken, New York 1964, p. 207).

III *The Mystery of Lawlessness*

1. Privately circulated untitled paper, 1972, pp. 1–2.

2. This is the teaching of the Second Vatican Council's Pastoral Constitution on the Church in the Modern World, *Gaudium et spes*, which, speaking of a wrong economic determinism, says: 'It too often happens that workers are made slaves of their work. This situation can by no means be justified by economic laws. The entire process of productive work, therefore, must be adapted to the needs of the person and to the requirements of his life' (no. 67).

3. Charles Birch, 'The Organic Image of Nature, Humanity, and God', *Anticipation* XXV, January 1979, p. 53.

4. 'Humanity, Nature and God', papers from the consultation in Zürich, July 1977, sponsored by the Working Committee on Church and Society of the World Council of Churches, published in *Anticipation* XXV, January 1979, p. 31.

5. Rosemary Radford Reuther, *To Change the World*, SCM Press 1981, p. 58. See footnote 2 above.

6. John Navone, *A Theology of Failure*, Paulist Press, New York 1974, pp. 59–60.

7. For example, the Fourth Lateran Council (1215): 'The devil and other spirits were indeed created by God good by nature, but they became evil by themselves' (DS 800); the Council of Florence (1442): 'It is firmly believed, professed, and taught, that no one conceived from man and woman was ever free from domination by the devil, unless through the faith of Our Lord, Jesus Christ' (DS 1347); the Second Vatican Council (1965): Pastoral Constitution on the Church in the Modern World, *Gaudium et spes*, section 13, Constitution on the Sacred Liturgy, *Sacrosanctum concilium*, section 6, and Decree on the Missionary Activity of the Church, *Ad gentes*, sections 3 and 9.

8. Paul VI, General Audience, 15 November 1972, quoted in *L'osservatore romano*, English language edition, 23 November 1972, p. 3.

9. See Matt. 8.23–7 and Luke 8.22–5.

10. See Matt. 14.22–3 and John 6.16–21.

11. See J. Heil, *Jesus Walking on the Sea*, Biblical Institute Press, Rome 1981, pp. 8–17 and 118–27.

12. See Heil, op. cit., pp. 42–3.

13. See Heil, op. cit., p. 97.

14. See Heil, op. cit., pp. 125–6.

15. See especially: M. Wakeman, *God's Battle with the Monster*, Brill, Leiden 1971; M. Delcor, 'Mythologie et apocalyptique', *Apocalypses et théologies de l'esperance*, ed. L. Monloubon, Cerf, Paris 1877, pp. 144–52;

T. Gaster, *Myth and Legend in the Old Testament*, Harper, New York 1969, vol. II, pp. 575–7 and 787–8.

16. See Job 7.12, 'Am I a sea or a sea monster that you set a guard over me?'

17. See Isa. 51.9–16.

18. He lied to Eve, and he is always 'a Liar and the father of lies' (John 8.44).

19. P. Teilhard de Chardin, 'Introduction to the Christian Life', *Christianity and Evolution*, Collins 1971, p. 163.

20. P. Teilhard de Chardin, *The Divine Milieu*, Collins 1960, p. 104.

IV Golden Calves and Golden Tables

1. E.g. Rom 1.11; 5.15–16; 6.23; 11.29; I Cor. 1.7; II Cor. 1.11.

2. *Lumen gentium*, no. 12; see also nos. 4 and 7.

3. On the theology of icons, see: P. Evdokimov, *L'art de l'icône. Théologie de la beauté*, Desclée de Brouwer, Paris 1970; P. Scazzoso, 'Il problema delle sacre icone', *Aevum* XLIII, 1969, pp. 304–323; *Dictionnaire de spiritualité*, vol. VII, articles on 'Icône' by T. Spidlik and P. Miguel (with a good bibliography), cols. 1224–1239.

4. It is a not uncommon error to confuse control by authority with service of an ideology. So, for example, Charles S. Mayer in 'Russian and Soviet Painting', *Artnews* LXXVI, 1977, pp. 68–70, thinks that both the icon tradition and contemporary Soviet art are 'less involved with the aesthetic concerns of the West than with the glorification of the Russian state' (p. 70). This is to miss the whole point of religious icons, which exist precisely to glorify God.

5. The Seventh Ecumenical Council, Nicea II, 787.

V Down to the Garden

1. Technically, this is a tropological interpretation, as distinguished from the literal, allegorical and anagogical interpretations; see R. Faricy, *Praying*, Villa, Dublin 1979, pp. 86–98, on spiritual exegesis.

2. *Gaudium et spes*, no. 39.

3. Ibid., no. 33.

4. Ibid., no. 34.

5. Ibid.

6. Ibid.

7. First Vatican Council, Dogmatic Constitution on the Catholic Faith, *Dei Filius*, canon 5 of chapter I.

8. Elizabeth of the Trinity, *Ecrits spirituels*, Seuil, Paris 1949, pp. 203–204.

9. G. M. Hopkins, in his poem 'Pied Beauty'.

10. Cf. Rev. 4.10; 7.11.

11. Ps. 100.1; 66.1; 98.4.

12. St Ignatius Loyola, *Spiritual Exercises*, no. 234.

13. Ibid., no. 236.

14. Ibid., no. 237.

15. See Jer. 31.37.

16. G. M. Hopkins, 'That Nature is a Heraclitean Fire and of the Comfort of the Resurrection'.

17. St John of the Cross, *Canciones entre el alma y el Esposo*, third song of the Bride.

18. J. M. Plunkett (1887–1916), 'I See His Blood upon the Rose'.